DK Illustrated Dictionary of
Mythology

KUAN YIN, THE CHINESE
GODDESS OF MERCY

NIDHOGG, THE NORSE
WORLD SERPENT

HAPY, THE EGYPTIAN GOD
OF THE NILE FLOOD

ISHTAR, THE MESOPOTAMIAN
GODDESS OF FERTILITY

GREEK HERO HERAKLES PRESENTS
THE ERYMANTHIAN BOAR TO THE
TERRIFIED KING EURYSTHEUS

JANUS, THE ROMAN
GOD OF BEGINNINGS

DK Illustrated Dictionary of
Mythology

Heroes, heroines,
gods, and goddesses from around the world

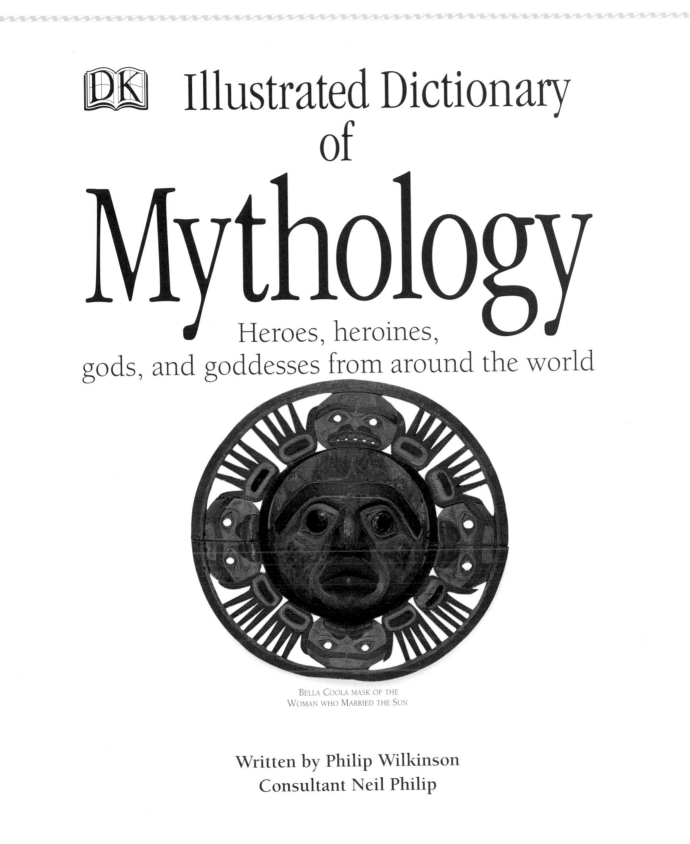

BELLA COOLA MASK OF THE
WOMAN WHO MARRIED THE SUN

Written by Philip Wilkinson
Consultant Neil Philip

GREEK HERO THESEUS SLAYS
THE EVIL SINIS

ASHUR, THE ASSYRIAN WINGED
GOD OF THE EARTH, AIR, AND SUN

SESHAT, THE EGYPTIAN
GODDESS OF WRITING

A DK PUBLISHING BOOK
www.dk.com

Produced for DK Publishing by
PAGEOne, Cairn House, Elgiva Lane, Chesham,
Buckinghamshire HP5 2JD

PROJECT DIRECTORS *Helen Parker, Bob Gordon*
EDITOR *Marion Dent*
DESIGNERS *Thomas Keenes, Melanie McDowell,
Suzanne Tuhrim*

FOR DORLING KINDERSLEY
MANAGING EDITOR *Jayne Parsons,*
MANAGING ART EDITOR *Gill Shaw*
PROJECT EDITOR *Maggie Crowley*
PRODUCTION *Kate Oliver*
PICTURE RESEARCH *Mariana Sonnenberg*
DK PICTURE LIBRARY *Sally Hamilton*
JACKET DESIGN *Mark Richards, Simon J. M. Oon*
US EDITOR *Will Lach*

First American edition, 1998
First American paperback edition, 2006
06 07 08 09 9 8 7 6

Published in the United States by DK Publishing Inc.,
375 Hudson Street, New York, NY 10014
Copyright © 2006 Dorling Kindersley Limited, London

Library of Congress Cataloging in Publication Data
Illustrated dictionary of mythology. – 1st American ed.
    p.   cm.
    Includes index.
    ISBN 0–7894–3413–X
    1. Mythology–Dictionaries.   I. DK Publishing, Inc.
BL303.I55   1998
291.1'3'03–dc21   98–22992
                                                                CIP

Color reproduction by Colourscan, Singapore
Printed and bound in Hong Kong

ASCLEPIUS AND HIS DAUGHTER HYGEIA,
GREEK DEITIES OF MEDICINE

BAAL, CANAANITE GOD OF
THUNDER, RAIN, AND FERTILITY

PARASHURAMA, THE SIXTH AVATAR OF VISHNU

RAMA, THE SEVENTH AVATAR OF VISHNU

KRISHNA, THE EIGHTH AVATAR OF VISHNU

CONTENTS

THE TERRIFYING HINDU
GODDESS KALI

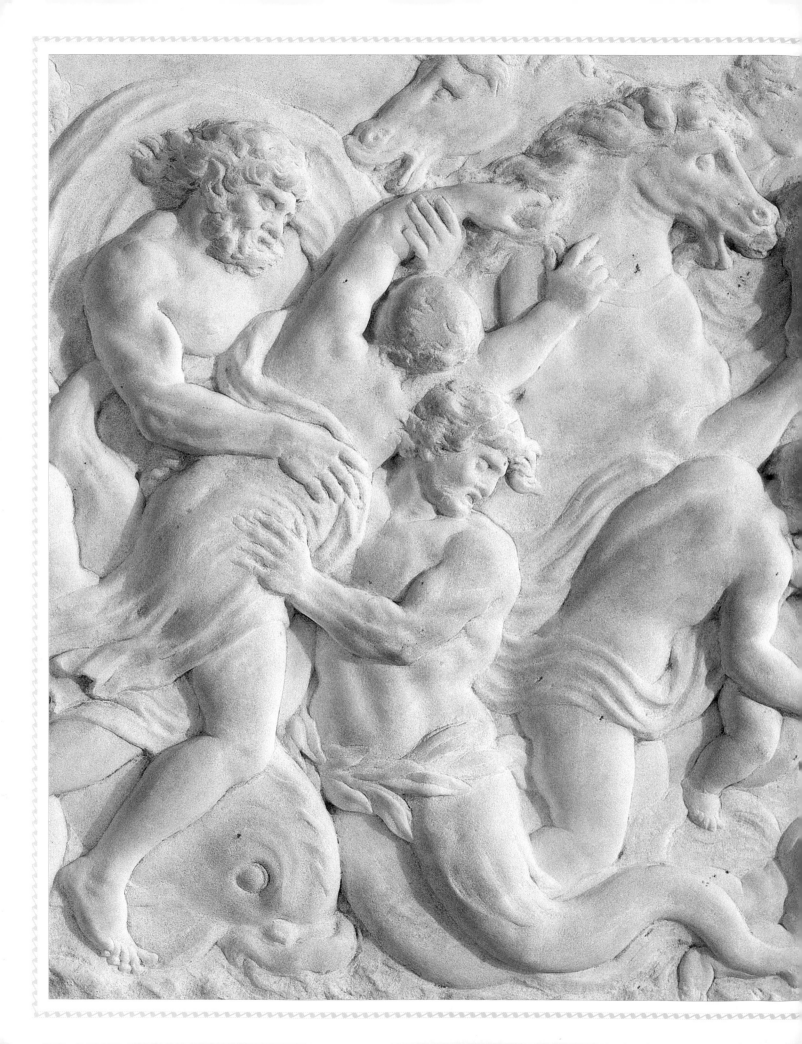

INTRODUCTION

Told and retold, constantly evolving from one generation to the next, the myths we know today form a living link to the creation of the earth and the origins of humanity. Around the world, from Asia and Africa to the Americas and Australasia, countless storytellers have passed down epic tales of adventuring heroes, the feats of the gods, and supernatural beings that attempt to explain creation and catastrophe, life and death.

MYTHS AND RELIGION

From time immemorial, early peoples all over the world have recounted these fantastical yet familiar myths. Before the advent of electric light, radio, and television, storytelling was often the only entertainment on long, dark evenings. Sometimes, the same stories also formed the basis of religion. Some of the myths in this book still form part of living religions, such as Shinto and Hinduism. Others belong to long-vanished cultures like ancient Egypt or the Roman Empire.

RECURRING THEMES

From Iceland to Africa, California to China, stories of the creation of the universe and humankind, epic journeys, battles of the gods, and the destruction of the cosmos recur, as do tales of great floods, trickster gods, and the hero's quest. A living part of all our heritage, myths are still some of the best stories of all time.

MEXICAN
BOY REENACTS
AZTEC JAGUAR MYTH

CREATION MYTHS

From the phases of the moon to the origin of humans, from the formation of canyons to the twinkling of stars, the world's creation myths describe how the universe was made and why it took its shape. Usually, these myths begin with chaos, which is often described as a dark void or an endless sea. From this void emerges a primal creator, or a pair of primal beings. These creators give shape to the universe, ordering the movement of the stars and moon, and creating the land – often by scooping up mud from the bottom of the ocean. In turn, these creators may then give way to other deities, who continue the process of creation by making plants, animals, and the human race.

When he was fishing in the ocean, Thor, the Norse thunder god, hauled up the World Serpent.

An ancient rock painting from Easter Island shows a bird-headed god holding the cosmic egg in its claws.

THE COSMIC EGG

Before the universe is made, the primal deities lie inert, waiting for the moment of creation. Myths often describe the gods or forces of creation confined inside a huge cosmic egg – at the crucial moment the egg cracks apart. One half forms the heavens, the other half becomes the earth. The creators emerge from the shell, to begin giving birth to the other gods or to create humanity. The Chinese, the Aztecs, the African Dogon people, and various Pacific tribes have myths of a cosmic egg, but there are many variations. The Chinese creator, Pan Ku, dies after the enormous effort of separating the heavens from the earth, but Rangi and Papa, the Maori heaven and earth, survive to produce deities and humans.

THE WORLD SERPENT

The enormous forces involved in creating the world are sometimes said to be caused by a powerful mythical beast – such as the World Serpent. This immense serpent lurks at the bottom of the ocean and contains creative energy in its mighty coils. An Egyptian myth tells how the snake Amduat was the source of all creation, since the sun god was born from its body. The World Serpent can incubate the cosmic egg, as in the early Greek story of the serpent Ophion, or it can be the Rainbow Snake, a creature common in both African and Australian myths – a creator of beasts or maker of rivers and oceans. In Hindu mythology, Vishnu rests on the serpent Ananta when a lotus appears from his navel. The flower opens and the creator god Brahma appears from within.

Using his foot as bait, the Aztec god Tezcatlipoca lured the Earth Monster, a kind of serpent, toward him. The Monster was injured after eating the god's foot and could not swim back down into the water, so the earth was made from her body.

FORMATION OF THE COSMOS

The first act of creation – the breaking of the cosmic egg or the birth of the primal creator – may take place quickly, but the rest of creation often happens over a long period. The process may involve many generations of gods and goddesses, whose families grow into a large pantheon in the heavens. The earth may then be made habitable, with the creation of rivers, oceans, plants, and animals, before humanity is created. In many mythologies, the process of creation is constantly repeated over a long period of time. Aztec and Native North American myths tell of a succession of different ages, in which the world is recreated in an endless cycle, repeated over and over with slight variations. These acts of creation produce an amazing variety of mythological worlds. For the Norse, the cosmos was seen as the great ash tree, Yggdrasil, which connected many different worlds – from Asgard, realm of the gods, to Midgard, the home of humans. In many African myths, the four cardinal directions were important, each one being associated with an element – water, earth, fire, and air – and there were often myths to explain the appearance of the universe.

In Aztec cosmology, each of the four cardinal directions had its own associations and colors. East, for example, was red and was equated with the realm of life and fertility. At the center stood Xiuhtecuhtli, god of fire, whose flames gave life to the cosmos.

The Greek mother goddess Gaia emerged from chaos with her consort, the sky god Uranos. Their children were rivers, trees, plants, and giants. Gaia and Uranos also made the Cyclopes from rock and fire.

PEOPLING THE WORLD

Humans often appear comparatively late in the creation process. The arrival of humankind can seem rather like an afterthought, coming after the more important work of creating the cosmos and the deities. The creation of people is usually a deliberate act by the gods and goddesses, which may be described in terms of some familiar human activity. For example, in many African myths, the gods mold the first people out of the earth, just as a potter makes vessels from clay. Chinese mythology describes the making of the first human in a similar way. Sometimes, the creation of humans is described as an accident, coming about as the result of some other action by the gods. In ancient Egyptian mythology, humans are created from the tears shed by the sun god when he is reunited with his children, Shu and Tefnut. A third account of human origins describes how people emerged from the soil. Native North American creation stories often tell of humans emerging through the earth from the previous world below. The ancient Greeks had a similar myth, describing the birth of Pelasgus, the first man, out of the soil of Arcadia.

The Chinese creator goddess Nü Wa had a human head and a serpent's tail. She made the first person by scooping up some mud and molding a copy of herself.

GODS AND GODDESSES

Each mythological system has its own pantheon, or collection of deities. Gods and goddesses may vary greatly from one culture to another. They may be related – one pair can be the parents of the gods – or they may have different parents who are created by one or more supreme deities. Deities may take human form, resemble animals, or be a hybrid of the two, but there are common themes. Gods often specialize in one area of activity, from warfare to agriculture, or take part of the cosmos or a certain region as their province. Deities often act like humans but on a much larger scale, with similar loves, friendships, conflicts, and jealousies.

This stone statuette from Anatolia, about 8,000 years old, may represent the ancient Great Goddess of Turkey.

THE GREAT GODDESS

Some of the most ancient statues found by archeologists are figures of ample, large-breasted females, who are thought to be early portrayals of the Great Goddess. Sometimes called the Earth Mother, or a fertility goddess often associated with the moon, the Great Goddess is one of the creators of the universe and a guardian of its fruitfulness.

DEITIES OF SUN AND RAIN

Early peoples did not understand what caused changing weather patterns, yet they depended on the weather for their survival – sun at the right time could produce a rich harvest, but a drought could destroy the crops and cause starvation. Wind, rain, and thunder were explained as the activities of various gods. Performing the right sacrifices for the gods ensured the best weather conditions and a plentiful supply of food. Most cultures have rain, sun, or thunder deities. In places where the sun's heat was felt most strongly, such as Egypt or South America, the sun god could be the most important deity of all. In areas where rain was scarce, such as the American Southwest, the rain gods were very important. With his booming voice that seemed to crack the heavens, the thunder god was also a powerful deity. Zeus, the Greek thunder god, was also king of the gods. The Norse thunder god, Thor, was terrifying in his anger, and was a great warrior against the giants.

The Egyptian goddess and creator figure Neith was an aspect of the Great Goddess, but later became a war goddess.

The Indian moon god Chandra traditionally rides across the sky in a chariot drawn by geese.

The Hindu sea goddess Tara rescued sailors who were at risk of shipwreck. She could change color according to her moods. When she was calm, she was green or white in color, when angry, she could be blue, red, or yellow.

GODS OF LAND AND SEA

Many gods began as local deities – the spirits of a particular place. Later, their fame would spread, or their myths combine with those of similar gods from nearby regions. And so hills, mountains, rivers, lakes, forests, and other parts of the earth had their own gods and goddesses. Their power and importance always depended on the type of culture and the local geography. For example, many landlocked peoples of central Europe feared spirits of the forests, who led people astray, or gods of streams and lakes, who could drag unwary travelers into the deep. For the Greeks with their maritime civilization, the sea god Poseidon had great power.

FERTILITY

Gods and goddesses of vegetation were common wherever agriculture was practiced. They were worshiped to make the fields fertile to ensure good harvests and plentiful food. Sometimes these deities were related to the sun and rain gods, but often they had a separate existence. There are deities, like Corn Woman from the American Great Plains or the Chinese Shen Nung, who taught people how to grow crops. Some deities, like Persephone, whose movements echoed the changing seasons, were essential to agriculture. But others, like Mesopotamian god Telepinus, were almost comic figures, whose silly sulks made the crops fail.

In his role as god of corn, Aztec god Quetzalcoatl was shown carrying five corncobs.

LOVE, MARRIAGE, AND CHILDBIRTH

The ability of people to form lasting relationships and bear children was important. Some of the most popular deities were the gods and goddesses of love. Figures such as the Greek Aphrodite, the Egyptian fertility goddess Aset, and the Mesopotamian Ishtar were well known and widely worshiped. The love gods' power was notorious and fast-acting – the Greek Cupid and the Hindu Kama fired arrows of desire at their victims. Gentler goddesses, such as the Egyptian Taweret and the Slavic Mokosh, helped mothers in childbirth.

The classical love god Eros (or Cupid) was known for his ruthlessness and could stimulate desire in his victims, whatever the consequences. He is often shown chasing or burning a butterfly – an example of his pointless cruelty.

HEROES AND TRICKSTERS

Strong, brave, and sometimes able to change their shape or perform other amazing feats, heroes and tricksters are some of the most popular characters in myth. They are usually male, although some Native North Americans, such as the Lakota, tell of heroines who taught people religious rituals. Heroes may be human or immortal; sometimes they are the offspring of a mortal and a god. Their deeds often had vital effects on human lives – heroes founded tribes and cities, killed monsters, provided the necessities of life such as fire, or taught skills such as metalworking.

The purest of King Arthur's knights, Galahad led the quest for the Holy Grail. In the Middle Ages, many Christians saw him as symbol of Christ himself, and a model for all Christians.

The Greek hero Theseus defeated the giant Procrustes, who used to torture his guests. Theseus stretched Procrustes on his own rack before cutting the giant to pieces.

EPIC JOURNEYS AND VALIANT QUESTS

The hero often had to go on a dangerous journey and had many exciting adventures along the way. Frequently, the journey was a quest for something important or valuable, like the Golden Fleece or the Holy Grail – or it may have been to a place of peril, such as a monster's lair. Heroes like Gilgamesh and Herakles even had to travel to the underworld. In ancient times, teachers and tribal leaders used these epic travels as examples for others to follow. Ancient Greeks admired the bravery of Herakles, while medieval Christians admired Galahad's virtue. Some of the world's greatest literature, such as Homer's *Odyssey* and the ancient Mesopotamian *Epic of Gilgamesh*, is based on the tales of brave heroes and their epic journeys.

One of the most famous heroic journeys was the voyage of Jason and the Argonauts to retrieve the Golden Fleece from Colchis. They battled with storms, sea monsters, Harpies, moving reefs, and other dangers on their travels.

WARRIOR HEROES

Many mythological heroes are military leaders and are brave in battle – they protect their people by leading them to victory against their enemies. There are numerous examples, from the Irish hero Cuchulain, who led the people of Ulster against the armies of Connacht, to Aeneas, who having slain his enemy Turnus and united the peoples of northern Italy, became one of the founders of Rome. Both these heroes became symbols for their people, and, years later, leaders would remind their followers of the hero's bravery when urging them on in battle. Most heroes had rather one-sided characters and were totally good, honorable, and always brave; however, a few heroes did have more complicated personalities. One of the best examples is the Hindu hero-prince Arjuna, who was a brave soldier and a highly skilled archer but disliked killing. Arjuna reasoned that he should not have to kill hundreds of people in battle, some of whom were his cousins. Another complex hero was Odysseus, who was not only brave but cunning. His clever inventiveness produced the giant wooden horse that won the Trojan War for the Greeks.

Vasudeva was an Indian prince who showed his devotion to Krishna by throwing himself on the funeral pyre when Krishna died and returned to heaven.

The archer Arjuna was helped by Krishna in his battle against his cousins – the Kauravas. Arjuna did not want to kill his cousins, but Krishna said to him: "Do your duty as a warrior, and do not fear to kill. I have already killed them."

TRICKSTER-HEROES

For many peoples, the culture hero who founded the tribe or gave people the essential skills of life was also a trickster. Such tricksters played a vital part in the mythology of the peoples of North America, Africa, and the Pacific islands. Often portrayed as an animal or a bird, the trickster used his wit to play jokes on his enemies. The stories of these tricks are highly entertaining, but they also have a serious side, because the trickster-hero can defeat the enemies of humanity, or use his skill to steal useful items like fire, from which humans can benefit. But the trickster was not always friendly – sometimes he played tricks on humanity. Even these jokes had their uses, since they reminded people how to deal with the mishaps and accidents of life.

From the American West to Mexico, Coyote is a renowned trickster and culture hero. A shape-changer, he took part in the creation of the world, but in some myths, Coyote was also responsible for the coming of death to the human race.

MYTHICAL MONSTERS

Dragons and sea beasts, elves and giants – the world's legends show a fantastic variety of mythical beings. Some were inhabitants or rulers of different areas on earth. Monsters with fins and scales ruled the seas, while the dwarfs of Norse mythology lived under mountains and mined gems and metals. Other mythical creatures resulted from the union of strange parents – rocks, air, or fire. Human encounters with such beings were often perilous, but some mythical beasts, like the dragons of Chinese myth, were usually kind to humans.

The hell of Japanese Shinto is known as Jigoku. It is inhabited by long-nosed goblins, who torture their victims mercilessly.

GIANTS

Colossal, lumbering creatures, many giants, such as the Norse Ymir and the Chinese Pan Ku, played an important role in the creation of the cosmos. Others, like the Titans and one-eyed Cyclopes of Greece, existed before most of the gods, although they played no part in the creation. In many myths, when the gods came into being, they took away the giants' power; the Cyclopes were banished to the underworld, but the trolls and frost giants of Norse mythology constantly waged war on, and stole from, their gods. Other giants plotted revenge, but usually had to be content with preying on unsuspecting humans.

Myths of the Kwakiutl people of the American Northwest tell of the giantess Tsonoqa. She carried off children to eat, but was often discovered because of her whistling.

This Russian mermaid is portrayed on a wooden relief that decorated a house. Surrounded by vegetation, she looks more like a fertility goddess than a terror to sailors.

MERMAIDS

Sailors from many parts of Europe told tales of mermaids – strange water-dwelling creatures, half-woman, half-fish. They came to the surface to lure mariners to their death with their beautiful song. Mermaids were said to live with their male counterparts (the mermen) in a luxurious undersea world, but they could not survive for long above water. Seeing a mermaid was supposed to be a sure sign that you would be shipwrecked. The Greek myths of the sirens, and of the beautiful love goddess Aphrodite, who was born from the foaming sea, are related to stories of mermaids.

SEA MONSTERS AND DRAGONS

Related to the mermaids was an entire race of other sea monsters and dragons. Many creation stories involve a giant snake coiled at the bottom of the ocean. Some of these beasts lived on after creation was completed – a source of both wonder and peril to sailors everywhere. Sea serpents coupled with other beings, to produce hybrid sea monsters with lions' heads and serpents' tails, or crocodiles' tails and eagles' heads. The most common of these hybrids were dragons, taking a variety of forms in different cultures. In the East, dragons were kind to humans – the Chinese still regard them as bringers of happiness, prosperity, and fertility, and dragon costumes are common at Chinese New Year celebrations. In Europe, dragons took more fearsome forms – fire-breathing monsters that attacked anyone who came near their jealously guarded treasure hordes.

In China, dragons were creatures of good fortune and bringers of rain, springtime, and fertility. They were also symbols of the emperor. This dragon image comes from a robe worn by an official at the imperial court.

The Greek sea creature Scylla began life as a beautiful sprite, but the jealous nymph Circe turned her into a hideous monster with dogs' heads growing from her waist. Scylla devoured passing seals, sea birds, fish – and sailors.

DWARFS, ELVES, AND MISCHIEVOUS SPIRITS

A group of oddly fascinating creatures that often caused chaos when they met mortals were neither human nor god. They ranged from ancient Greek nymphs to the mischievous spirits and goblins of central Europe, who are blamed for breaking crockery or making nighttime noises. They were often local spirits, associated with a particular stream, lake, or woodland. Some, such as the dwarfs and elves of northern Europe, looked like miniature humans. The wise dwarfs were highly skilled miners and metalworkers and lived underground to avoid sunlight. They could cause mischief, but were loyal to their friends. The more slender delicate elves created havoc among humans, by swapping babies in their cradles, spreading diseases among cattle, and bringing on bad dreams. Other cultures have similar beings. Some Native American myths tell of small, clever, sometimes helpful spirits, like dwarfs, while the Irish leprechauns and European fairies are similar to elves.

In China, the mythical Qilin personified justice. It used its horn to strike the guilty, but allowed the innocent to go free.

ANIMALS AND PLANTS

From birds that soar through the air to reptiles lurking just
beneath the water's surface, animals have always inhabited realms
alien to humans. Animals, such as bulls, jaguars, lions, and serpents,
can also be much stronger, more ferocious, and better hunters than
people. It is not surprising that gods and goddesses often took animal
form and that many peoples regarded animals as having great spiritual
power. Awesome creatures, like the Thunderbird of North America or
Mexico's Jaguar God, are remote from humans, but demand people's
respect. But many myths show that the natural world is much closer to
humankind. The ancestors of the Australian Aborigines took animal
form, and in places from western Africa to Mesoamerica, people were
said to have an animal double.

*Sobek, the Egyptian crocodile
god, was known as a symbol
of the strength and power
of the pharaoh.*

THE POWER OF THE BIRDS AND THE BEASTS

Some cultures, awed by the power and variety of the creatures around
them, gave the bodies of animals and birds to nearly all of their gods and
goddesses. Many of the deities of ancient Egypt – from Hathor the cow to
Sobek the crocodile – had animal forms, while others took human shape,
but kept the head of a bird or beast. Numerous African peoples, and
many of the Native North American tribes, look upon everything in
the natural world as having a spirit. Animal deities abound in
these cultures, and range from tricksters, such as Rabbit,
Coyote, and Tortoise, to the gods and goddesses of
wind and storm, like the great Thunderbird. Some
creatures occur again and again with similar
associations in different parts of the
world. The earth goddess is often
portrayed as a cow, and is
valued for her nourishing
milk. The ocean can be
represented by the snake,
an animal both powerful
and dangerous,
suggestive of the sea
monsters that early
sailors imagined were
just below the ocean's
surface, waiting to cause
tidal waves and capsize
their ships. Sky gods were
frequently birds, but the bull,
with its thunderous roar, was
sometimes a god of the heavens.

*Many Native North American peoples told of the
Thunderbird – a deity of thunder, lightning, rain,
and fire who was also often seen as a creator
god. This Thunderbird mask was made by the
Kwakiutl people of northwestern North America.*

*The jaguar was worshiped by most of the ancient peoples of Mexico,
from the earliest Mexican civilization – the Olmec – onward.
The jaguar's strength and skill as a hunter were widely admired.*

PART HUMAN, PART ANIMAL

Hybrids of humans and animals appear in many myths. Although they were often terrifying monsters, they had special powers. A being that was part animal and part human could use its unique knowledge of the animal world, and pass it on to other gods and goddesses or mortals. Hybrid creatures, such as the ancient Greek centaur Chiron, were thought to be especially wise, and they were also said to have the ability to heal the sick or foretell the future.

HUMAN AND ANIMAL

Some of the most dramatic myths involve the relationship between humans and animals. Often the animal is a monster who must be killed for the good of the world. Other animals had magical powers or were fascinating in their own right, making men and heroes want to possess them. Greek hero Herakles' labors involved capturing several beasts, including a monstrous boar and a giant bull. Often there is a closer human-animal relationship.

Catching the Cretan Bull was one of Herakles' Twelve Labors. The Cretan King Minos vowed to sacrifice to the sea god Poseidon anything that appeared in the sea, but when Minos saw the bull appear in the water, he kept the beast for himself.

This Aztec ornament is made as a two-headed snake, a symbol of the rain god Tlaloc. The snake, like the rain, has always been associated with fertility.

Many cultures – from North America to Australia – look back to a time when animals were our ancestors or when animals and humans had the same status, even speaking the same language. Northwestern American myths tell how people and polar bears lived together, and one story even tells of a woman who married a bear.

TREES AND PLANTS

Forests are dark, mysterious places filled with woodland spirits who are often blamed when people get lost among the trees. If a person cut down a tree, guardian spirits, like the ancient Greek Hamadryads, would exact a more severe punishment – a Thessalian prince was stricken with endless hunger when he felled a grove of trees. But the magical qualities of trees went beyond this. For the Norse, the entire cosmos was built around Yggdrasil, a gigantic ash tree. For many people, smaller plants, like wheat, rice, and corn, had more prominence in myth. These cultivated crops are life itself to farming peoples and have their own gods and goddesses. Farmers performed special ceremonies to the plant deities at key moments in the growing cycle, notably at sowing, planting, or harvesting times. Such rituals ensured that the deities of crops such as wheat, grapes, lotus, corn, and pomegranate were some of the most powerful spirits of all.

The corn, or maize, plant was so important to the people of ancient Peru that it was sometimes portrayed in human form.

The lotus flower plays a role in myth from Egypt to India. Here, the Naga King Varuna sits on a lotus flower lifted by serpents.

ENDINGS

Will the world end one day? What happens when we die? Are there such places as heaven or hell? World mythologies answer these important questions with stories about the soul, the underworld, and the end of the world. The prospect of death is frightening, but myths show that it is possible to have a brush with death and survive. Many stories involve gods, like Mesopotamian Tammuz, who are brought back to life, and heroes, like Greek Orpheus, who return from the underworld. Some myths tell how souls live on in another world, or come back to life in a different body. The history of the cosmos is treated in a similar way. The world may end, but it can be reborn, with new deities, so that life can carry on.

Anubis, the jackal-headed god of mummification, presides over the embalming of a corpse – the most important of the ancient Egyptian rituals connected with the afterlife.

A Japanese Buddhist depiction of hell shows a mirror to reflect sinners' bad deeds and scales to weigh their souls – the tongues of liars are torn away.

THE AFTERLIFE

In many myths, the soul has to go on a journey to the next world. This voyage is often dangerous and tests the soul – a successful journey will ensure a good reception in the underworld. Early people buried grave goods, such as weapons or food, with their dead, to help them on their way to the afterlife. For those who had not lived a good life on earth, punishments were often in store. The Egyptians imagined that the unworthy souls were gobbled up by the goddess Ammut, the Devourer of the Dead. In the Japanese tradition, Jigoku, a hell with 16 different regions, awaits to punish the sinful. Those who lived good lives were usually treated well in the next world. The best treatment of all was given to heroes. The Norse said that the souls of heroes went to join Odin in Valhalla. For the Greeks and Romans, dead heroes went to dwell in the Elysian Fields for an afterlife of pleasure. In many African cultures the attitude to the next world was very different. It was seen as a place where souls waited until the time came for them to be reborn on earth in another form.

Matsya, the fish avatar of the Hindu god Vishnu, protected Manu, the first man, during the great flood.

The Aztec sun god Tonatiuh carries on his back a symbol representing an earthquake. The Aztecs believed that the Fifth (or present) Era would end with an earthquake.

WORLD DISASTERS

Stories of catastrophes helped people to make sense of natural disasters such as fires and floods. Myths of a great flood that envelops the earth are told all over the world. Mesopotamia, India, China, Mexico, and Australia all have flood stories. In many cases, the flood comes because people have misbehaved or made the gods angry. Only those who are chosen by the gods, like the Mesopotamian hero Utnapishtim or India's first man Manu, are warned and can take action to survive – usually by building a ship. World catastrophes can occur as the result of forces such as fires and earthquakes. Indian, Chinese, and Native American myths speak of cosmic fires. Fire often purifies the cosmos, wiping out evil and making the world a better place when the flames die down.

A Viking plaque shows a pair of wolves swallowing the old sky in part of the destruction of the world that occurs at Ragnarök, the last great battle.

ENDINGS AND BEGINNINGS

A cosmic disaster, such as a fire, flood, or war, is often described as bringing about the end of the world, but life does not stop. Usually, a new world grows from the ashes of the old world, and a new cycle of life can begin. One of the most famous examples of this death and rebirth of the cosmos occurs in Norse mythology. After Ragnarök, the last great battle, most of the old gods are killed, but a new pantheon and world order emerge. Sometimes this pattern of death and rebirth is repeated over and over. The Aztecs believed that they lived in the Fifth (or present) Era, and that previously the world had been destroyed, in turn, by jaguars, a hurricane, a fire, and a flood. Some Native North American peoples also have myths in which a number of worlds are destroyed in a series of disasters brought on by the gods. On the other side of the world, Hindu traditions evolved notions of cycles of creation and destruction, taking place over a vast time-scale. Stories like these helped people come to terms with natural disasters, enabling them to explain these events as part of a larger plan for the world, and giving them some hope that a new and better world could emerge from the most terrible catastrophes.

Between the destruction of the old world and the creation of a new world, the Hindu god Vishnu rests with his wife Lakshmi on the serpent Ananta, which represents eternity.

19

WESTERN ASIA

The first civilizations grew up in the area called Mesopotamia, between the Tigris and Euphrates Rivers, c.5000 BC. The people who lived there – the Sumerians, Babylonians, and Assyrians – built cities, established religions, devised the first system of writing, and wrote down their myths.

PEOPLES AND GODS

The myths of Sumeria depict a world largely in harmony. The gods control life on earth and are served by humankind. The later myths of Babylonia and Assyria, which involve the same gods but give them different names, show a more turbulent world and raise

questions about life, immortality, and why natural disasters occur. Persian myths tell of the struggle between good and evil as shown by twin deities – the destructive Angra Mainyu and Ahura Mazda, the Lord of Light.

MYTHS AND HISTORY

GILGAMESH AND THE LION

Some western Asiatic myths were based partly on historical fact. For example, the *Epic of Gilgamesh* includes a huge flood that actually occurred in Mesopotamia, c.4000 BC.

SUMERIAN AND BABYLONIAN NAMES

SUMERIAN	BABYLONIAN	SUMERIAN	BABYLONIAN
An	Anu	Inanna	Ishtar
Enki	Ea	Nanna	Sin
Enlil	Enlil or Ellil	Utu	Shamash

CREATION MYTHS OF MESOPOTAMIA

SEVERAL DIFFERENT CREATION STORIES have come down to us from the time of the great civilizations of Mesopotamia. Many of the clay tablets on which the stories were written have been lost or broken, so some myths are not complete. The usual creation myth begins with the primeval sea. In Sumer "the sea" or "the myth" was called Nammu. In Babylonia the world began with a pair of deities, Apsu and Tiamat. Unlike the Sumerians, the Babylonians also gave Marduk, their city god, a prominent place in the creation story. In both civilizations, the higher gods were born of the primeval sea. They created the earth and the heavens, and produced humans to act as their servants.

Marduk   *Tiamat*

TIAMAT
The goddess Tiamat, shown as a female dragon, was the saltwater ocean and the embodiment of primeval chaos. She founded a dynasty of deities with **Apsu**, who was killed by **Ea**. In revenge, she attacked Ea with fearsome monsters. When **Marduk** killed Tiamat, one-half of her body became the sky, the other the earth.

AN (ANU)
The god of the sky, or Lord of the Heavens, was known as An, son of **Nammu** to the Sumerians, but Anu, descendant of **Apsu** and **Tiamat**, to the Babylonians. One story tells that Anu won his kingdom in a game of dice with his sons **Ea** and **Enlil**, with the result that Enlil won the earth, Ea the sea, and Anu the sky. As the supreme god of the universe, An was thought to stand aloof and all-knowing in the sky. He was an impartial judge of both gods and mortals, and was respected for his sense of justice. He was also the keeper of the bread and water of eternal life, which made the gods immortal.

SKY GOD AN

NAMMU
In some Sumerian myths, the primeval sea is known as the goddess Nammu. Her written name used the same Sumerian symbol as the word for "sea." Described as "the mother who gave birth to heaven and earth," her children were **Ki**, goddess of the earth, and **An**, the sky god.

LAHMU
The union of **Tiamat** and **Apsu** produced a series of godly couples, each more powerful than the one before. The first of these couples was Lahmu and Lahamu. Little-known figures, their role was as parents of the next generation, Anshar and Kishar. Sometimes Lahmu was portrayed as a serpent, but some statues show him in human shape. This bearded figure shows a later, Assyrian form of the god – Lahmu the Hairy.

APSU
In the beginning, there were only Apsu, the primeval ocean of fresh water, and **Tiamat**, the saltwater ocean. The waters of Apsu circled the earth, which was like a floating island. Springs of fresh water also bubbled up through the earth's surface. Apsu was a male being who united with Tiamat to create the first Babylonian gods and goddesses, culminating in **Anu** and **Ea**, who produced the supreme god **Marduk**.

KI
The earth goddess Ki produced the great gods of Sumer through her union with the sky god **An**. Ki was mother of **Enlil**, the god of farming, the arts, and civilization; **Enki**, the god of wisdom; and several other prominent gods. Therefore, she became known as mother of the gods. One story tells how she and **Enlil** created humanity, so Ki also became the mother-figure of mortals.

LION, ISHTAR'S
SACRED ANIMAL

Enlil

ENLIL
The god of earth and air was called Enlil. He was responsible for separating heaven from earth and was the father of humankind. Enlil invented the pickax, which he gave to mortals so that they could build the great cities of Mesopotamia. But Enlil also had a violent side. In his role as wind god, he was probably responsible for the great flood.

LION
The lion was the sacred animal of **Ishtar**, the Babylonian goddess of fertility and sexual love, and pictures of lions adorned the Ishtar Gate at the entrance to Babylon. Daughter of **Anu** or **Ea**, Ishtar was the star of the evening and was identified with the planet Venus. To the Sumerians, she was called Inanna. As star of the morning, she was also the goddess of war.

NANNA

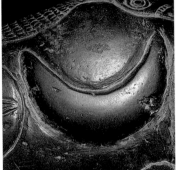

After being raped by **Enlil**, the harvest goddess Ninlil gave birth to the moon god Nanna, whose symbol is a crescent moon. As a punishment Enlil was sent to the underworld, so Ninlil followed him there. When Nanna was born in the darkness of the underworld, his light was pale and cool. As he journeyed across the sky, monsters from the nether world would chase him, causing his monthly waning. He waxed big again as a result of sacrifices made by his worshipers on earth.

GUARDIAN SPIRITS

Many western Asiatic gods acted as guardians of mortals. For example, **Ea** advised **Utnapishtim** to build a boat when the great flood was coming, to save humans from destruction. But the best known protectors of humans were the genii, or guardian spirits. These were lesser gods who guarded humanity against evil, and acted as messengers of the gods. Carvings of genii, placed at the gates of temples and palaces, were portrayed as hybrid creatures with both animal and human features. Genii were often bulls with wings and human heads, but could sometimes appear as eagle-headed humans. There were also evil genii: part human, part lion.

SPHINXLIKE GUARDIAN SPIRIT

Utu / *Sun disk, symbol of Utu* / *Worshiper*

Ea, god of wisdom / *Winged goddess Ishtar* / *Shamash, the sun god*

UTU (SHAMASH)

The son of the Sumerian deities **Nanna** and Ningal, Utu (Shamash in Babylonia) was the sun god and also the god of justice. Each day he emerged from a door in the Mountain of the East and rode his chariot across the sky to the Western Mountain. At night he traveled eastward underground so that he was back in the Eastern Mountain by morning. The sun's rays were said to be his judgments. They could burn evildoers or make a net in which to trap the unjust. In the Sumerian myth of the great seven-day flood, Utu appeared in a bark to bring back the light after the storm.

NINMAH

According to one myth, Ninmah, the goddess of birth, created humans because **Nammu** and the other gods and goddesses wanted servants. **Enki**, the god of wisdom, showed Ninmah how to fashion the humans out of clay.

EA (ENKI)

The god of wisdom, Ea was also known as Enki. He kept copies of the heavenly laws that laid down the rules of social life and religion. **Ishtar**, jealous of the power Ea had as keeper of the laws, stole the tablets on which the laws were written.

NINHURSAG

In Sumerian myth, the earth mother Ninhursag was responsible for curing the sickness of **Enki**, the god of wisdom and the waters. When Enki coupled with Uttu, the goddess of horticulture, eight plants were produced. Before Uttu could name them, Enki ate all eight plants and became very sick. Ninhursag then created eight deities, each one corresponding to a different ailing part of Enki's body. Enki was cured, and the eight deities were said to be his children.

DOGLIKE DRAGON, SYMBOL OF MARDUK

Grain, produced by Ashnan

ASHNAN

The gods created Ashnan, the grain goddess, and her brother **Lahar**, the cattle god, to provide them with food and clothes. But the pair neglected their duties, so the gods created humans to serve them.

LAHAR

When the cattle god Lahar and his sister **Ashnan** were sent to earth, the land prospered. **Enki** gave Lahar plants and animals and provided Ashnan with oxen and plows. One day Lahar and Ashnan got drunk and quarreled over who owned what. **Enlil** and Enki had to step in to make peace.

MARDUK

Worshiped in Babylon, Marduk, son of **Ea**, was one of the chief creator gods. He took a major part in the battle between the primal creators, **Apsu** and **Tiamat**, and the younger deities, such as Ea and **Enlil**, who won Marduk's support by promising him great power if he would help them fight Tiamat. Tiamat, turning herself into a serpent, swallowed Marduk, who had become the wind. Marduk killed Tiamat, creating heaven and earth from her body, and becoming the supreme deity of the Babylonian pantheon.

MESOPOTAMIAN UNDERWORLD

AFTER DEATH, people went to the underworld, which was beneath the ground, guarded by seven gates. As the deceased passed through each gate, they took off part of their clothing, so they eventually arrived naked in the underworld. Here the souls of the dead lived, jumbled up together in a state of uncomfortable confusion – few had even a bed or fresh water. A group of deities ruled the underworld. Chief of these were Ereshkigal, queen of the underworld, and her husband Nergal. They were assisted by Namtaru, god of disease, and Belili, sister of Tammuz, god of vegetation.

CYLINDER SEAL SHOWS ZU BEING JUDGED BY EA AFTER STEALING THE TABLETS FROM ENLIL

Adapa broke the South Wind's wings because a storm blew up

ISHTAR

Gilgamesh faced the Scorpions at the gate of Mashu in the underworld

ADAPA
Created by **Ea**, Adapa (the first man) had great strength and wisdom and invented language. Once when he was sailing on the Euphrates, the South Wind blew on his ship and almost sank it. Adapa tore off the wind's wings in rage. When the sky god **An** sent Adapa to heaven to explain his actions, Ea advised him not to eat or drink anything there. Adapa refused the food and drink of immortality offered by An, thus condemning humanity to mortality.

THE SCORPIONS
Half-man, half-dragon, the terrible Scorpions guarded the gate of Mashu in the underworld, which protected the rising and setting sun. Their glance could kill a man, but **Gilgamesh** was two-thirds divine. When questioned by the Scorpions, Gilgamesh, in mourning over his friend **Enkidu**'s death, said he had traveled here to find his ancestor **Utnapishtim** to ask him why men must die.

ISHTAR AND TAMMUZ
Goddess of fertility and sexual love, Ishtar was also the goddess of war. Her husband Tammuz was the god of vegetation and spring. According to one myth, Ishtar descended to the underworld and tried to seize the throne from her sister **Ereshkigal** but was killed, causing the springs on earth to run dry. **Ea** rescued her and allowed her to leave the underworld on condition that she send a substitute. So for half of the year she sent Tammuz to the underworld; for the other half she sent his sister Geshtinanna.

ZU
The Assyrian storm god, Zu, had a birdlike form. In one story he stole the stone Tablets of Creation from **Enlil** and became ruler of the world. The war god Ninurta confronted Zu about his crime. He threw storm clouds around Zu, tore off his wings, and beheaded him, then took the Tablets and returned them to Enlil. Zu was finally put on trial before the supreme god **Ea**.

LILITH
A terrifying goddess of death, Lilith appeared in Hebrew myths, but may be the same figure who featured in earlier Mesopotamian myths as the fertility goddess Ninlil, consort of **Enlil** and mother of their child, the moon god **Nanna**. Lilith took the form of a demon who stole babies and turned them into demons.

LILITH, GODDESS OF DEATH

NERGAL
Enlil's son Nergal, a huge, bull-like figure, caused chaos wherever he went. Nergal raped **Ereshkigal**, queen of darkness and ruler of the underworld, then ran back to heaven, pursued by Ereshkigal. Seeing that this would cloak the universe in darkness, **An** sent Nergal back to the underworld, to rule jointly with Ereshkigal.

STONE MACEHEAD DEDICATED TO NERGAL

ERESHKIGAL
The elder sister of **Ishtar**, Ereshkigal ruled the underworld. While Ishtar represented light, Ereshkigal was the goddess of darkness and, therefore, invisible to mortals. However, she could turn parts of herself into visible monsters – part vulture, part snake – and could send these terrifying creatures to earth.

ETANA
The mythical ancestor of the kings of Mesopotamia, Etana was selected by the gods to rule on earth. He and his wife could not have children, so Etana set out on the back of an eagle to obtain the plant of birth from **Ishtar**, goddess of fertility, in heaven. But before he reached Ishtar, Etana became dizzy and fell off the eagle to earth.

THE EPIC OF GILGAMESH

The world's oldest work of literature, this epic dates back to 2000 BC or even earlier. It tells how the people of Uruk, in Mesopotamia, asked the gods to do something about their tyrannical king Gilgamesh. The story relates the king's adventures with Enkidu, the wild man the gods sent to subdue him, and describes Gilgamesh's search for immortality.

CARVING OF EPIC HERO GILGAMESH WITH A LION

GILGAMESH AND ENKIDU FOUGHT THE BULL OF HEAVEN

HUMBABA

ENKIDU
The gods sent Enkidu, a warrior of great strength, to tame **Gilgamesh**. But the king tricked Enkidu by persuading a woman to seduce him and show him the ways of civilization. Then Gilgamesh and Enkidu wrestled in a great test of strength, but neither won; they became firm friends and roamed the world together. **Ishtar** sent the Bull of Heaven to destroy Gilgamesh. Enkidu helped Gilgamesh kill the bull, but died in the king's arms. The gods had said that one of them must die to avenge the bull.

Animals entered the boat Utnapishtim built to survive the great flood

UTNAPISHTIM
After **Enkidu**'s death, **Gilgamesh** tried to find everlasting life. Utnapishtim, survivor of the great flood and the only human who had been granted eternal life, told Gilgamesh that his only hope lay in picking a plant called "never grow old" from the seabed. Gilgamesh found the plant, but it was eaten by a snake. Since then, snakes have renewed their skin by shedding it, but humankind, having lost the plant of everlasting youth, dies.

HUMBABA
The epic relates how **Gilgamesh** and **Enkidu** slew two monsters. The first was Humbaba, a fire-breathing beast that the gods hoped would kill them both. But Enkidu held the monster while Gilgamesh stabbed it in the neck. Enkidu also helped Gilgamesh kill a bull sent by **Ishtar** after the king refused her amorous advances.

GILGAMESH
Gilgamesh was the son of a mortal man and the goddess Ninsun – the source of his great strength. He terrorized his people, but later, when he had freed the earth of vicious monsters and saw his friend die in his arms, he became a sympathetic character, one of the first great heroes.

HADAD
The thunder god Hadad, whose name means Crasher, was the most important Syrian god. From his mountaintop home, his voice sounded in the heavens, and his thunderbolt could bring death and destruction. He was identified with the Canaanite storm god **Baal**.

ASHUR
The greatest of the Assyrian gods, Ashur was god of the earth, air, and sun. The Assyrians adapted Babylonian mythology, making him the husband of **Ishtar**. But his most important role was that of war god, and prisoners of war were paraded through the streets in his honor.

ASHUR, THE ASSYRIAN WINGED GOD OF THE EARTH, AIR, AND SUN

OTHER WESTERN ASIAN GODS

As well as Assyria, Sumeria, and Babylonia in Mesopotamia, Western Asia was home to several other distinctive ancient civilizations. The Canaanites lived along the eastern Mediterranean coast (in what is now Syria, Israel, Lebanon, and Jordan); their civilization flourished during the 14th century BC. The Hittites built up a large empire from their base in central Turkey around the same period. The Persians, from modern Iran, built up their own empire during the sixth to fourth centuries BC. Each culture had its own mythology, with its own creation myths, fertility deities, and stories of rivalries between the gods.

THE PERSIANS

Ahura Mazda (Ormuzd) and Angra Mainyu (Ahriman), constantly struggling forces of good and evil, were the two main figures in Persian mythology. Ahura Mazda was defended by a group of spirits (the Amshaspends), while Angra Mainyu was followed by demons called the Daevas. Sinners followed Angra Mainyu, but moral people wanted evil banished.

THE HITTITES

Hittite myths involved hundreds of gods. Many were fertility deities and gods of farming and weather, both vital to this agricultural people in Turkey's arid, rocky terrain.

TESHUB
Thunder god Teshub overthrew Kumarbi, father of the gods, and became a powerful Hittite deity. Waving his thunderbolt, he rode across the sky on a bellowing bull.

TELEPINUS

TELEPINUS
Teshub's son, Telepinus, the god of agriculture, went into hiding and the crops began to fail. When found, he flew home on an eagle, and the crops began to grow again.

HANNAHANNAS
The mother goddess Hannahannas was important in finding **Telepinus**. She suggested sending a bee to look for him. The other gods ridiculed the suggestion, but the bee found Telepinus, sleeping, and stung him awake.

HANNAHANNAS

KAMRUSEPAS, GODDESS OF HEALING AND MAGIC

KAMRUSEPAS
The goddess of healing and magic, Kamrusepas was called on by the other gods to heal **Telepinus** after he was stung by **Hannahannas'** bee. Only after Telepinus was restored to health could he return home.

Ahura Mazda spread his protective wings over the world

AHURA MAZDA
Ahura Mazda, the sky god, means Wise Lord. As god of wisdom, he could prophesy the future. He was also god of fruitfulness and fertility. His opponent was **Angra Mainyu**. Atar, Ahura Mazda's son and fire of the sky, fought Angra Mainyu's three-headed dragon, Azhi Dahaka. Atar banished the dragon, who threatened to eat the world. It was said that the beast would return at the end of the world to wipe out a third of its population.

ANGRA MAINYU, GOD OF DARKNESS

YIMA
In Persian myth, the first man was Yima. He was created immortal, but his immortality was taken away when he gave his people meat to eat. As punishment, Yima had to gather plants and animals of all kinds and shelter them. At the end of time, Yima would return to repopulate the earth.

ZOROASTER
The prophet Zoroaster lived in about 1000 BC. He founded the Zoroastrian religion, which sees the world and its history in terms of the struggle between the gods of good and evil, **Ahura Mazda** and **Angra Mainyu**. Zoroaster is thought to have written the Gathas, hymns that form part of the Avesta, the Zoroastrian sacred book. He encouraged every person to follow Ahura Mazda, so that Angra Mainyu would be defeated and good would reign in the world.

ZURVAN
The Persian primal creator Zurvan (Time) had both male and female qualities and bore the twins **Ahura Mazda** and **Angra Mainyu**. Zurvan said that the firstborn would be the most powerful – whereupon Angra Mainyu ripped his way out of Zurvan's womb first. Zurvan then said that this power would last 1,000 years, then evil would be destroyed.

ANGRA MAINYU
Ahura Mazda's twin brother, Angra Mainyu, was the sky god's opposite – the deity of darkness, destruction, sterility, and death. He struggled against goodness and attempted to overthrow Ahura Mazda. Angra Mainyu made a horde of destructive monsters, together with hazards such as whirlwinds, storms, and diseases, to threaten Ahura Mazda's creation of the universe and humankind.

THE PROPHET ZOROASTER

GAYOMART, THE FIRST MORTAL HUMAN

GAYOMART
The first mortal human being was Gayomart, who was created from the light by **Ahura Mazda**, and in turn became the creator of all subsequent human life. Gayomart, the father of the first human couple, spread his seed on the earth. It stayed in the ground for 40 years, then sprouted to produce **Mashya and Mashyoi**, the ancestors of the human race. **Angra Mainyu**, the god of darkness, was jealous of this act of creation and murdered Gayomart.

MASHYA AND MASHYOI

MASHYA AND MASHYOI
As soon as they came to life, Mashya and Mashyoi, the ancestors of all humans, rejoiced in the world and its creation by **Ahura Mazda**. But they forsook Ahura Mazda when evil **Angra Mainyu** whispered to them that he was the true creator. When Angra Mainyu killed **Gayomart**, Mashya and Mashyoi were so taken in by the god of darkness that they did not defend Gayomart or complain to Ahura Mazda. As punishment for their treachery, Ahura Mazda made them mortal.

MITHRA
Mithra (or Friend), **Ahura Mazda**'s son, was one of the most popular Persian gods. God of wisdom and warfare, Mithra could aim his deadly weapons and let loose his terrifying wild boar, Verethraghna, at the enemies of Ahura Mazda. Also a sun god, Mithra drove his chariot across the sky each day to banish the powers of darkness. In Roman times, he became Mithras, a deity popular with Roman soldiers, who sacrificed bulls in his honor.

Mithras slayed the bull

THE CANAANITES
In 1929, a collection of clay tablets was discovered in northwestern Syria, at Ras Shamra, the ancient Canaanite city of Ugarit. For the first time, details of ancient Canaanite myths, current in 1360 BC, were revealed. Many stories concerned Baal, a fertility god, and El, the supreme god, great and wise.

BAAL
God of thunder and rain, Baal was also the main fertility god. Baal's myth tells how he disappeared and reappeared, like the seasons. Baal overcame **Yam**, the sea god, and fought with **Mot**, the god of death. Baal appeared to be killed, but he revived long enough for fertility to return to earth.

BAAL, GOD OF FERTILITY

ASHERAT
Asherat was the Canaanite fertility goddess and one of the wives of **El**. Her name has several forms, including Ashtart and Astarte. She may be related to the Mesopotamian goddesses Inanna and **Ishtar**. Portrayed as a woman or a cow, the milk from her breasts streamed across the heavens to form the Milky Way.

YAM
The god of the sea and disorder, Yam wanted to rule the earth. Yam challenged **Baal** for supremacy, but Baal tore him limb from limb and scattered his remains. Baal proclaimed his dominance over the waters of life.

ASHERAT, GODDESS OF FERTILITY

SAOSHYANT
Persian myth says that at the end of the world, **Angra Mainyu**'s evil will be banished. Saoshyant (the Savior) will come, sinners will be purged of their sins, and the dead will be resurrected.

SAOSHYANT, SAVIOR OF THE WORLD

EL
The Father of Gods and Men, El was the supreme creator in Canaanite mythology. He married two fertility goddesses, Anath and **Asherat**, and became father of the Canaanite gods. A somewhat remote figure, he was usually portrayed sitting on his throne, wearing the horns of a bull, symbol of his great strength.

MOT
The god of death, Mot was associated with sterility and drought, making him an opponent of **Baal**, god of fertility and rain. When defeated by Baal, Mot was banished to the underworld.

EL, THE SUPREME CREATOR

SHAPASH
The Canaanite goddess of the sun, Shapash, was known as the Torch of the Gods. Intervening in the struggle between **Baal** and **Mot**, she persuaded the latter to release Baal.

AQUAT
The Canaanite mortal Aquat owned a bow that represented the arch of the heavens. Anat, the warrior goddess, killed Aquat to get it, but the bow went to the underworld, bringing darkness to the earth. **El** retrieved the bow and returned light to the earth.

ANCIENT EGYPT

On the banks of the Nile River, the ancient Egyptians created a civilization that lasted almost continuously from 3000 BC to the first century BC. Ruled by kings and priests, their society developed a highly complex mythology, with hundreds of gods and goddesses.

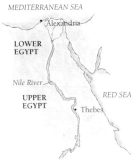

A VARIETY OF GODS

Most Egyptian myths began as stories of local gods or goddesses. The early Egyptians believed that every living thing had a spirit, and many deities were the spirits of local animals, such as the falcon or the crocodile, or geographical features, such as the Nile. As an area became more influential, its deities were adapted and worshiped farther afield, often retaining the animal identities, such as an animal's head on a human body.

SCARAB, SYMBOL OF RISING SUN

THE SUN GOD

The sun god was the most powerful of all Egyptian deities and took many forms – from a soaring bird of prey to a scuttling scarab beetle. The Egyptians believed that their king, or pharaoh, was an incarnation of the sun god – that the god had come to life.

MYTHS AND RITUAL

Egyptians believed that they went to join the gods in the next world when they died, so they preserved the bodies of their dead by mummification, for use in the afterlife. Mummification was surrounded by solemn rituals, and many gods and goddesses presided over these ceremonies.

EGYPTIAN CREATION

THE SCRIBES OF ANCIENT EGYPT recorded several different accounts of the creation. The priests of Memphis believed the god Ptah created the world, while at Heliopolis, the sun god Atum, or Ra, was worshiped as the creator. Atum began as the chaos that existed before the gods. His name means "the all," indicating that he contained the essence of all future creation, male and female, divine and human. His first act of creation was to gather himself together into the shape of a human. He then spat or sneezed into the void to create Shu and Tefnut, the ancestors of the gods. In another version of the story, Atum took the form of a huge snake that would shed his skin at the end of time. Atum would emerge to create the world all over again, so beginning a new cycle of existence.

THE SUN GOD RA-ATUM IN HIS BOAT

Sun disk

Coiled cobra-goddess, showing the god's power to bring about death instantly

Falcon head

RA-ATUM

The sun god emerged from the water or from a primeval lotus flower. There are several different stories about his role as creator. In one myth, Ra wept, and from the tear that fell to earth, humanity was created. In another story, the god's daily journey to the underworld deprived the earth of light, so he created the moon god **Thoth** to shine at night. Ra was also identified with Atum, and was thought to be the father of **Shu** and **Tefnut**, the parents of the gods.

BENBEN STONE

This stone, set up in the temple of the sun god at Heliopolis, represented the mound that was pushed up out of the ground on which the sun god stood and performed his first acts of creation. Its shape, a shortened, pyramid-topped obelisk, inspired many structures in Egyptian art and architecture, including the pyramids.

In the act of creation, Shu, the god of air, holds Nut aloft, separating her from her twin Geb, god of the earth

Nut, goddess of the sky

TEFNUT, SHOWN WITH A RAM'S HEAD

GEB AND NUT

The twins Geb, god of the earth, and Nut, goddess of the sky, were the children of **Shu** and **Tefnut**. At birth, they were locked together in an embrace; their grandfather **Ra-Atum** told Shu to separate them. When Shu did this, he pushed Nut upward to form the great arch of the sky, with her hands and feet resting on the four points of the compass. Every day the sun god made his journey from dawn to dusk across this arch. Nut's body protected the cosmos from the chaos above; thunder was explained as her laughter. When Shu separated Geb from his sister, Geb was forced downward, creating the flat earth. As god of the earth, Geb was partly responsible for land fertility and crop growth.

SHU

Shu, the god of air and father of the twins **Geb** and **Nut**, was created by **Ra-Atum**. He was sometimes shown kneeling, holding the sky on his shoulders. His main task was to bring the sun god and the pharaoh to life at the beginning of each day. Also a torturer, he slaughtered the souls of the wicked in the underworld.

TEFNUT

Daughter of **Ra-Atum**, sister of **Shu**, and mother of **Geb** and **Nut**, Tefnut was the goddess of moisture. Siblings Tefnut and Shu became the first divine couple. Tefnut was shown in several forms, including a lioness and a pair of spitting lips. In the form of a serpent, she coiled around the pharaoh's scepter. As long as she stayed, there would be no drought. She is also said to have built a pool for the pharaoh, so he could wash his feet.

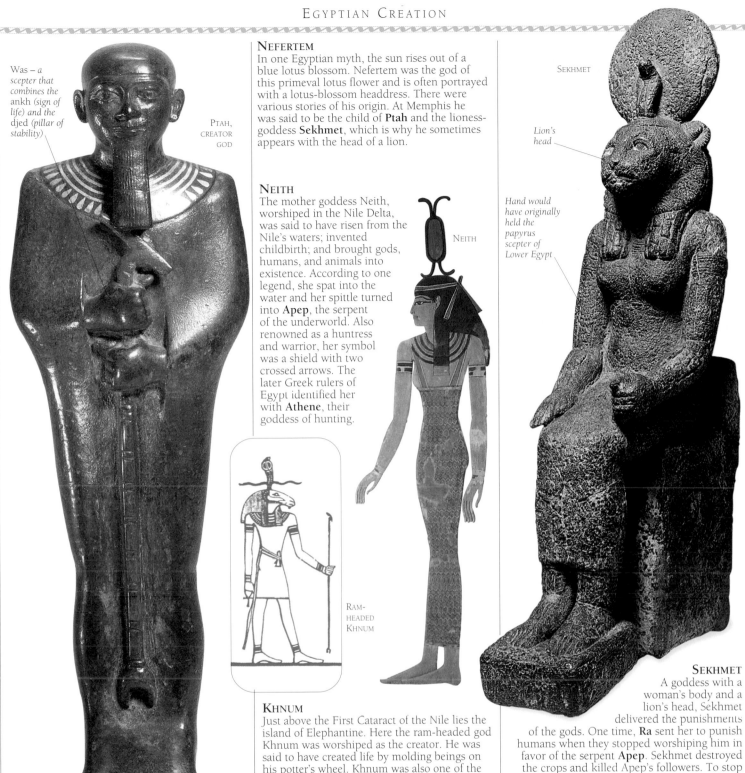

Was – a scepter that combines the ankh (sign of life) and the djed (pillar of stability)

PTAH, CREATOR GOD

NEFERTEM
In one Egyptian myth, the sun rises out of a blue lotus blossom. Nefertem was the god of this primeval lotus flower and is often portrayed with a lotus-blossom headdress. There were various stories of his origin. At Memphis he was said to be the child of **Ptah** and the lioness-goddess **Sekhmet**, which is why he sometimes appears with the head of a lion.

NEITH
The mother goddess Neith, worshiped in the Nile Delta, was said to have risen from the Nile's waters; invented childbirth; and brought gods, humans, and animals into existence. According to one legend, she spat into the water and her spittle turned into **Apep**, the serpent of the underworld. Also renowned as a huntress and warrior, her symbol was a shield with two crossed arrows. The later Greek rulers of Egypt identified her with **Athene**, their goddess of hunting.

NEITH

RAM-HEADED KHNUM

KHNUM
Just above the First Cataract of the Nile lies the island of Elephantine. Here the ram-headed god Khnum was worshiped as the creator. He was said to have created life by molding beings on his potter's wheel. Khnum was also one of the gods of the Nile, controlling the annual flood by opening the sluice gates in the caverns of **Hapy**, the god of the flood.

SEKHMET

Lion's head

Hand would have originally held the papyrus scepter of Lower Egypt

SEKHMET
A goddess with a woman's body and a lion's head, Sekhmet delivered the punishments of the gods. One time, **Ra** sent her to punish humans when they stopped worshiping him in favor of the serpent **Apep**. Sekhmet destroyed the crops and killed Apep's followers. To stop her, Ra's servants tricked her into drinking beer, dyed red like blood, so that she got drunk, lost interest in killing, and eventually fell asleep.

PTAH
The priests at Memphis worshiped the creator god Ptah (the Sculptor), son of Nun and Naunet, spirits of the primeval seas. He created the first gods by thinking them into existence and then naming them. The heart, which the Egyptians took to be the origin of thought, and the voice, representing the god's breath of life, were seen as Ptah's continuing presence on earth. Using his sculptor's art, Ptah then formed beings out of wood, stone, and metal. He may also have created the pharaoh Ramesses II from metal. As a result, he became the god of craftspeople and was sometimes shown as a blacksmith.

BENU BIRD
The Benu Bird, commonly depicted as a heron, was said to have risen from the waters at the beginning of time. It was usually described as one of the forms taken by the sun god, and was worshiped at the temples of **Atum** and **Ra**. Like the sun god, the Benu Bird, a symbol of rebirth, created itself. Later, the ancient Greeks linked it to their own self-creating bird, the phoenix, which rose from its burned-out ashes every 500 years.

EGYPTIAN UNDERWORLD

THE ANCIENT EGYPTIANS believed that the souls of the dead went to Duat, the Egyptian underworld, to join the god Osiris and the souls of other dead people. But not every soul was admitted to Duat. Each had to appear before a committee of 42 assessor gods in the throne room of Osiris. These gods questioned the deceased about their life, accusing them of numerous crimes and sins. The deceased denied all the accusations, and each person's heart (their conscience) was weighed on a large set of scales, to see if they were telling the truth. The truthful were admitted to Duat.

Hieroglyphs on head say "Nephthys, Lady of the Mansion"

NEPHTHYS
The daughter of **Geb** and **Nut**, Nephthys was the sister of **Isis**, **Osiris**, and **Seth**. Nephthys' marriage to Seth produced no children, but the jackal god **Anubis** was her son by Osiris. After the death of Osiris, Nephthys left the evil Seth and mourned with her sister Isis. Egyptian artists often portrayed the two mourning goddesses as a pair of hawks. At Egyptian funerals, two women usually took the roles of Isis and Nephthys, grieving over the mummy and sometimes even wearing hawk masks.

Osiris holding the crook and flail, the scepters of kingship

ISIS HOLDING HORUS, HER CHILD BY OSIRIS

Isis wears a crown of cow horns and a sun disk

Black coat represents the color of the corpse after mummification

ANUBIS THE EMBALMER WITH A MUMMY

OSIRIS
The supreme god, Osiris brought plants and the seasons to the earth. He taught humans how to farm and instructed them in the arts of civilization. As the eldest child of **Geb** and **Nut**, he ruled on earth, becoming the first pharaoh. But his brother **Seth** was jealous of his power and decided to kill Osiris. Seth made a beautiful wooden chest and announced that he would give it to anyone who fitted inside. It was a perfect fit for Osiris, and when he got inside, Seth nailed down the lid and threw it into the Nile. Osiris' wife, **Isis**, pulled the god's body out of the Nile and briefly revived it. But Seth got hold of it again and tore it into bits. Each piece was buried in a different part of Egypt. After his death, Osiris became god of the underworld.

ANUBIS
Son of **Nephthys** and **Osiris**, the jackal-headed Anubis was the god of embalming and of cemeteries. When Osiris died, Anubis embalmed the body and wrapped it in bandages, making the first mummy. Later, he joined Osiris in the underworld. Here he became the deity who presided over the ceremony of weighing the heart, in which the deceased's heart was weighed to find out whether that person had led a good life. Anubis then took the souls of those who passed this test to be judged before Osiris himself.

ISIS AND HORUS
The faithful wife and sister of **Osiris**, Isis created the Nile from her tears. Isis was also the mother of Osiris' child, Horus, the falcon-headed sky god whose eyes were the moon and the sun. He was conceived when Isis turned herself into a hawk and beat her wings to try to bring the breath of life back to Osiris. Horus guided dead souls in the underworld, and was a protector of the pharaoh, who took the title the Living Horus, given to all Egypt's rulers.

SOKAR
The hawk-god Sokar made silver bowls in which the deceased bathed their feet. Sokar also mixed the herbs and spices to make the ointments used in funerary rites. Because he was a craftsman, Sokar was often identified with the god **Ptah** (the Sculptor) in many Egyptian texts. Known as the Lord of the Mysterious Region, Sokar is often shown traveling through his realm in a boat.

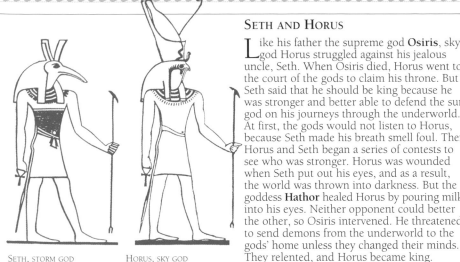

SETH, STORM GOD   HORUS, SKY GOD

SETH AND HORUS

Like his father the supreme god **Osiris**, sky god Horus struggled against his jealous uncle, Seth. When Osiris died, Horus went to the court of the gods to claim his throne. But Seth said that he should be king because he was stronger and better able to defend the sun god on his journeys through the underworld. At first, the gods would not listen to Horus, because Seth made his breath smell foul. Then Horus and Seth began a series of contests to see who was stronger. Horus was wounded when Seth put out his eyes, and as a result, the world was thrown into darkness. But the goddess **Hathor** healed Horus by pouring milk into his eyes. Neither opponent could better the other, so Osiris intervened. He threatened to send demons from the underworld to the gods' home unless they changed their minds. They relented, and Horus became king.

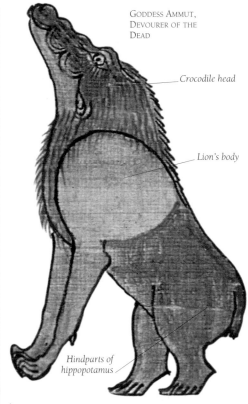

GODDESS AMMUT, DEVOURER OF THE DEAD

Crocodile head

Lion's body

Hindparts of hippopotamus

THOTH

God of the moon and of wisdom, Thoth is portrayed with the head of a bird – the ibis. Accounts of his ancestry vary: some texts say that he was the son of **Seth**, others that his father was **Ra-Atum**. He invented many intellectual pursuits, such as astronomy, geometry, magic, medicine, and music, but he was best known as the inventor of writing. In the underworld, Thoth's tasks included writing down the names of all the souls and looking after the scales in which the hearts of the deceased were weighed.

Thoth's curved beak represents the crescent moon

Maat wore a headdress with a single ostrich feather

THREE FORMS OF MAAT

MAAT

The goddess of truth, harmony, and justice, Maat, the daughter of **Ra** and the wife of **Thoth,** wore a single ostrich feather in her headdress. In the underworld, the deceased's heart was weighed against this feather. The heart of an honest person would be as light as Maat's feather, but if the heart was troubled with past sins, the balance would be tipped and the heart was given to **Ammut**, the Devourer of the Dead.

SESHAT WORE A HEADDRESS WITH A SEVEN-POINTED STAR

AMMUT

The goddess Ammut stood by the scales when the hearts of the deceased were weighed at the entrance to the underworld. If the deceased had led a wicked life and was not fit to survive into the next world, she ate the heart, giving rise to her title, Devourer of the Dead. Her form incorporated three of the most feared animals of ancient Egypt – the head of a crocodile, the body of a lion, and the hindparts of a hippopotamus.

SESHAT

Known as the Queen of the Library, Seshat was the wife of **Ptah**, god of writing. She is portrayed wearing a headdress adorned with a seven-pointed star and a panther-skin robe. She acted as scribe to the gods, noting down the taxes they collected and the spoils they won in battle.

WEPWAWET

Portrayed with the head of a jackal, Wepwawet, Opener of the Ways, guided the deceased's soul through the underworld and assisted in weighing the heart. He was also guardian of the pharaoh and sponsor of royal conquests.

APEP

The snake god Apep lay coiled in the underworld, powerful enough to annihilate his victims. Each day, when the sun god traveled through the underworld, Apep attacked the god's boat. The dead, led by **Seth**, a god of unsurpassed strength, succeeded each night in defeating the serpent, allowing the boat to pass through. But each day Apep revived, ready to attack the sun god once more and terrify all comers with his bellowing roar.

Every night, the snake god Apep fought with the sun god

FERTILITY AND ANIMAL GODS

THE ANCIENT EGYPTIANS lived in a hostile environment. Only a narrow strip of land on either side of the Nile River was suitable for farming and human settlement; beyond this was desert. People relied on the flooding of the river to keep the soil fertile. But the Nile and its banks, though life-giving, were full of dangerous creatures, including crocodiles, hippopotamuses, and lions. It is not surprising that the Egyptians gave their gods the characters of these powerful creatures, and no wonder that many of these gods were concerned with the fertility of the soil, and the health and fertility of the Egyptians themselves.

Full moon

KHONSU, MOON GOD

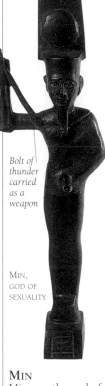

Bolt of thunder carried as a weapon

MIN, GOD OF SEXUALITY

RENENET
A cobra goddess, Renenet presided over the harvest, as well as weaning infants. She was also guardian of the pharaoh. Her gaze could frighten away all enemies, but it also had the power to help crops grow, to ensure prosperity and food for the pharaoh and the people of Egypt.

MESHKENET
Goddess of childbirth, Meshkenet took the form of a tile with a female head, like a brick on which women squatted when they gave birth. She also sat next to the scales in the underworld when the deceased's hearts were being weighed, and she helped at the rebirth of the soul in the next world.

HAPY
Hapy was the god of the Nile floods. He lived in a cave near the cataract of the river. It was his job to keep the land on either side of the river fertile and he did this by scattering seeds into the water as it flowed out of the sluices onto the land. Hapy was portrayed with large, pendulous breasts and a fat belly, both of which are symbols of fertility. His headdress was adorned with water plants.

Headdress adorned with reeds

Fat belly and large breasts symbolize fertility

HAPY, GOD OF THE NILE FLOOD

BES, AN UGLY-LOOKING DWARF, FRIGHTENED AWAY EVIL SPIRITS

KHONSU
A moon god, Khonsu was often portrayed with the moon on his head. Sometimes he had a hawk's head, to show that he is a god of the skies. His name means "wanderer," because of the moon's journey across the sky. He was said to grow from child to adult during the first half of the month, before gradually shrinking back to a child's size as the moon waned.

MIN
Min was the god of sexuality. He was worshiped as a creative force, but was also destructive – some stories describe him as a god of war carrying a thunderbolt. Priests and pharaohs offered flowers to Min in the hope that he would bring fertility to the Nile Valley. They also made offerings of lettuce, Min's sacred plant, thought to be an aphrodisiac.

BES
The Egyptians thought that ugly creatures could frighten away evil spirits. Bes was an ugly-looking but friendly dwarf who liked fun and music. Sometimes he is shown playing the tambourine or the harp. Together with **Taweret**, he looked on when women were giving birth. A popular god, it was thought that Bes brought good fortune to married couples and their families, so people often decorated their houses with images of Bes.

HATHOR
Guardian of women (especially women in childbirth) and protector of lovers, the cow goddess Hathor was the daughter of the sun god **Ra-Atum**. She suckled the god **Horus** and came to his aid when **Seth** put out his eyes; she later married him. Her milk then became the food of the gods. Papyrus was her sacred plant, since cattle are often seen in the swamps by the Nile, where papyrus reeds grow.

TAWERET
The goddess Taweret protected women during childbirth. She had the head of a hippopotamus, a lion's limbs, the tail of a crocodile, and human breasts. Like **Bes**, her forbidding appearance was thought to frighten away evil spirits. A pregnant woman would wear a charm of Taweret on a cord around her neck; a new mother might place some of her milk in a special vase made in the shape of the goddess when reciting a good luck spell.

Hathor

Papyrus, the sacred plant of cow goddess Hathor

TAWERET, PROTECTRESS OF WOMEN

SOBEK, THE
CROCODILE GOD

SOBEK
The crocodile god Sobek, son of **Neith**, represented the power of the pharaoh. Crocodiles could move with great speed and had powerful jaws, attributes that recalled the skill and strength of the pharaoh in battle. There were many temples to Sobek in the Nile Valley and his worship continued when the Greeks ruled Egypt; they named a city Crocodilopolis in commemoration of the god. Real crocodiles, sacred to Sobek, were adorned with jewels and mummified when they died.

APIS
One incarnation of the god **Ptah** was the bull god Apis. The priests at Memphis kept a real bull that was thought to be the god's living image. The bull lived in luxurious accommodations near the temple of Ptah, and at regular festivals the Egyptian upper classes were allowed to come and view the bull. When the bull died, it was mummified in a solemn ceremony and buried in underground catacombs.

APIS, THE BULL GOD

Headdress in the form of a vulture

MUT, SURROGATE
ROYAL MOTHER

Bastet was first portrayed as a lioness, but later as a cat

BASTET
Daughter of **Ra**, Bastet was a goddess of sexuality and childbirth. After about 1000 BC, sculptors started to portray her as a cat. She was worshiped at Bubastis in the Nile Delta, where many thousands of dead cats were mummified in her honor. Egyptians revered all cats and believed they were lucky. If there was a fire, it was thought that the cats would rush into it, drawing the flames away from the people in the house.

SERKET, THE
SCORPION
GODDESS

MUT
The wife of Amun, Mut (or "mother") could appear as a cow or a cat, since sometimes she was identified with **Hathor** or **Bastet**. With Amun and her son **Khonsu**, she made up the trio of gods worshiped at the city of Thebes. The Egyptians believed that when an earthly queen was pregnant, Mut came to earth, turned herself into the queen, and gave birth to the new pharaoh-to-be.

SERKET
With many different roles, mainly linked to her power to repel evil, Serket protected the throne of the pharaoh. She was present during funerary rites (when she was responsible for the inner organs, removed during the embalming process), and she guarded a dangerous area in the underworld. Serket also prevented the serpent **Apep** from attacking the sun god's ship in the underworld.

THE SPHINX
In Egypt the **Sphinx**, with its man's head and lion's body, symbolized the strength and spirit of the pharaoh. It was a peaceful creature, except when the king was threatened by his enemies. It was also an incarnation of the sun god, hence its title, **Horus** of the Horizon. Many sphinxes still stand on guard outside the temples of Egypt. The most famous is the Great Sphinx at Giza, probably carved around 5,000 years ago. It is 240 ft (73 m) in length.

THE GREAT
SPHINX AT GIZA

INDIA

For thousands of years, the myths that form the basis of the Hindu religion were passed down by word of mouth. In the telling and retelling, countless variations evolved, making Indian mythology, in which order comes from chaos, one of the most complex of all the world's mythologies.

THE SACRED TEXTS

The stories of the Indian gods and heroes were written down in sacred texts in the regional Sanskrit language – the *Vedas* were composed c.2000 BC; the *Mahabharata* and *Ramayana*, 200 BC–AD 200; and the *Puranas*, AD 250–1700.

FOUR-HEADED
BRAHMA

FEW AND MANY

Of the hundreds of Hindu deities, several stand out as very important. Among the gods, a triad of prominent figures – Brahma, Shiva, and Vishnu – have special significance. Many Hindu goddesses are seen as incarnations of the Great Goddess, Mahadevi. Above them all is Brahman, the eternal unifying force.

OTHER TRADITIONS

India has other religions, such as Buddhism and Jainism, which developed during the sixth century BC. Many myths involve the Buddha, from his miraculous birth to the earth tremors when he died. Followers of Jainism see the cosmos as a gigantic human figure, at the head of which are 24 great prophets, or tirthankaras.

BRAHMAN AND THE TRIAD

OF THE HUNDREDS OF INDIAN GODS, three are of supreme significance and are known as the Triad: Brahma, the Creator; Shiva, the Destroyer; and Vishnu, the Preserver, who mediates between the other two. These deities have a great cosmic importance and exist in a time-scale quite different from human time. One *kalpa* (one day and night of Brahma) is made up of 4.32 billion human years. Within this infinity, human life exists as a constant cycle of creation, destruction, and rebirth.

Between creations of the cosmos, Vishnu rests on the serpent Ananta (representing eternity)

BRAHMAN

There is more diversity in Hinduism than in any other religion. But with all this variety there is also a single unifying force – Brahman, the eternal unity of the universe. Brahman is not a god; he is the soul of the universe and the essence of life. The creator god **Brahma** began originally as an incarnation of Brahman.

BRAHMA

The creator god Brahma was born from a lotus that grew from a seed in **Vishnu**'s navel. There are several stories about Brahma creating the world. In one, he made a god that symbolized his ignorance of what creation would be like. When Brahma threw this god away, it became night and produced terrifying demons called yakshas and rakshasas. To compensate, Brahma began to make goddesses and gods. In another tale, Brahma created the beautiful goddess **Sarasvati**, who became mother of the universe.

BRAHMA

ANANTA

The serpent Ananta, the Endless (also called Vasuki and Shesha), lay coiled at the bottom of the sea, where **Vishnu** rested on his coils. Fire from his mouth was said to destroy the world at the end of each cosmic era.

PRAJAPATI

One of the earliest Indian deities, Prajapati created himself from the primeval ocean. When he saw the emptiness around him, he wept, and his tears became continents. He made gods, demons, and human beings from his own body. Later his personality merged with that of **Brahma**.

Disk denotes cycle of creation and destruction

Mace symbolizes power

SHIVA

The Destroyer Shiva is an all-knowing punisher of the wicked. He has four arms, and a third eye on his forehead from which fire comes, making everyone shrink away in fear. At the end of each age of the universe, fire from Shiva's eye will destroy gods and mortals alike. Although he was a fearsome figure, Shiva was also a protector. Violent yet protective, active yet thoughtful, creator and destroyer, Shiva took many forms and had many names.

Flame of destruction symbolizes rebirth

FOUR-ARMED, FOUR-FACED DANCING SHIVA, THE DESTROYER

Lotus means purity

Conch shell symbolizes origin of existence

VISHNU

The third member of the Triad, Vishnu preserves the universe and is its stability. According to early Vedic myths, Vishnu encompassed the entire universe in three strides, showing earth, middle air, and heaven to be fit places for gods and mortals. When the world is under threat from some force of evil, Vishnu appears in one of his **avatars** (incarnations) to protect it. Hindu myths select ten avatars (from his countless many) as being of special importance and power. Vishnu was also identified with the great column that Hindus believe holds up heaven and connects it to the earth.

VISHNU, PRESERVER OF THE UNIVERSE

THE TEN AVATARS OF VISHNU

MATSYA
The fish avatar, Matsya saved **Manu**, the first man, from the great flood.

KURMA
The tortoise avatar, Kurma supported the sacred Mount Mandara on his back while the gods and demons churned the ocean, from which the sun and the moon arose.

VARAHA
The boar avatar, Varaha used his tusk to lift earth (depicted as a beautiful woman) out of the ocean, after earth fell in.

NARASIMHA
The man-lion avatar, Narasimha killed Hiranyakashipu, the invulnerable demon who had brought terror to the world, by disemboweling him.

VAMANA
The dwarf avatar, Vamana transformed himself into a giant, to trick the demon Bali and his followers, who had taken over the world.

PARASHURAMA
The sixth avatar, a brave human warrior, carried a battle-ax given him by **Shiva**. He killed many enemies, such as the hundred-armed **Arjuna**.

RAMA
The seventh avatar was the human lord Rama. A major figure in Hindu mythology, he is the hero of the *Ramayana*, an epic poem on the feats of **Vishnu**'s incarnations.

KRISHNA
The eighth avatar, Krishna slew the bull-demon Arishta, the horse-demon Keshin, and Kamsa, evil ruler of Mathura. Krishna is worshiped as a god in his own right.

BUDDHA
The Buddha, the great religious teacher who founded Buddhism, is regarded as the ninth avatar of **Vishnu**. He defeats enemies by guile, not physical strength.

KALKI
The tenth and future avatar, Kalki will end current evil and begin a new, golden age.

Garuda was sometimes portrayed as an eagle, other times as half-eagle, half-human

VISHNU RIDING GARUDA, THE DEVOURER

Conch shell

GARUDA
The Devourer Garuda was **Vishnu**'s steed. His aunt Kadru, mother of snakes, captured his mother, Vinata, mother of birds, and said she would release her sister only if she was given the elixir of the gods. Garuda flew to the mountain where the elixir was kept and brought it to Kadru, who released Vinata. The snakes licked the grass where the elixir lay. The sharp blades of the grass cut the serpents' tongues, which have been forked ever since.

NANDIN, SHIVA'S BULL MOUNT

NANDIN
Shiva rode a milk-white bull, called Nandin. This bull was a symbol of strength and also of fertility, and so was a powerful vehicle for the god. Shiva sometimes rode into battle on the back of Nandin, who was the protector of four-legged animals. A statue of a recumbent Nandin was often placed opposite the chief temples honoring Shiva, so that Nandin could gaze at the image of his master. Bulls are still regarded as holy in India because of their link to Shiva.

HINDU GODS AND HEROES

THE HINDU MYTHS FEATURE MANY HEROES, whose adventures are told in epic poems and who are sometimes incarnations of the gods. There are also demons, such as the nagas, rakshasas, and asuras. None of these beings originally had the gift of immortality, but the gods decided that they wanted to be immortal. Vishnu had the idea of creating an elixir of life (a liquid that made the drinker immortal) by throwing herbs and precious stones into the sea of milk and churning it up. He uprooted Mount Mandara, wrapping the serpent Vasuki (Shesha or Ananta) around the mountain. The gods pulled one end of the snake, the asuras pulled the other, to produce the churning motion and create the elixir of immortality.

INDRA

INDRA
The rain and thunder god, Indra, was king of the gods in the early Hindu myths. He got his power when he killed Vritra, a serpent who had swallowed the world's water. When Vritra died the water poured, causing the monsoon and giving life. Indra rode on an elephant.

ELEPHANT-HEADED GANESH, GOD OF GOOD LUCK

Ganesh used his missing tusk as a pen

AGNI, GOD OF FIRE

SKANDA
Six-headed Skanda (Karttikeya) is god of armies and battles. He began as six children, born from six sparks from **Shiva**'s eyes. Shiva's wife **Parvati** loved her six sons so much and hugged them so tightly that they turned into a baby with six heads. Usually Skanda is shown riding a peacock, followed by a vast army.

SIX-HEADED SKANDA

AGNI
The god of fire, Agni is sometimes depicted with seven arms and a goat's head. Agni's fire takes many forms – from lightning to the spark of inspiration – and makes all things pure, which is why Hindus burn the bodies of the dead. When people die, Agni sends smoke from their funeral pyre to heaven, together with their souls.

GANESH
The god of good luck, Ganesh is the son of **Shiva** and **Parvati**. Several stories tell how he came to have an elephant's head. In one of the most popular, Parvati wanted a son to guard her from troublesome visitors, so she created Ganesh out of scrapings from her skin and placed him outside her quarters. When Ganesh stopped Parvati's husband Shiva from entering, Shiva cut off Ganesh's head. Parvati was devastated, so Shiva replaced the head with that of the first animal to come along – the elephant.

ARJUNA
Son of the god **Indra** and a mortal queen, Arjuna was an accomplished archer and played a major role in a great war between the Kauravas and the Pandavas. This was recounted in the epic poem, the *Mahabharata*. Not just a warrior, Arjuna was also a thoughtful man. His conversations with **Krishna** are related in the *Bhagavad Gita*, part of the *Mahabharata*.

Shesha the serpent protecting Vishnu

PORTABLE SHRINE TO VISHNU, FOR HINDUS' DAILY WORSHIP (OR *PUJA*)

Vishnu   Balarama   Krishna

BALARAMA
The god **Vishnu** placed two hairs in the womb of Devaki, a mortal. One grew into **Krishna**, the other became Balarama. Balarama was a human hero with superhuman, god-given powers. He waged fearsome wars using various weapons to slaughter his enemies. But he could also be a rather amusing figure, with a liking for drink and comic banter with Krishna.

BHARATA
Bharata's parents were King Dasharatha and Queen Kaikeyi. When Dasharatha decided to abdicate, he gave the throne to Bharata's brother, **Rama**, and was dismayed that his wife wanted Bharata to be king and to send Rama into exile. But Bharata nobly refused to take the title of king and ruled instead as Rama's prince regent.

CHANDRA
The moon god Chandra (Radiant) was born during the churning of the sea of milk. He is also known as Soma – the name of the gods' sacred drink. Chandra's waning came about because each day the gods took some Soma to drink; his waxing occurred when the god Surya brought water to restore his strength.

THE RAMAYANA

This great Hindu epic was written down between c.200 BC and c.AD 200. Among a wealth of other stories, it tells of the adventures of its hero, Rama – his victories against a race of demons called the rakshasas, his marriage to the beautiful Sita, the abduction of Sita by Ravana, and Sita's eventual rescue by Rama, Lakshman, and Hanuman. After his adventures, Rama returned home and reigned for the next thousand years.

Ravana, King of the rakshasas

THE BATTLE OF SRI LANKA (CEYLON)

Lakshman, Rama's loyal follower

Rama

RAMA

The lord Rama was the seventh avatar of **Vishnu** and heir to King Dasharatha. He married **Sita**, the beautiful daughter of Janaka, king of Videha. He spent 14 years in exile while **Bharata** ruled in his place, and it was during this time that Sita was kidnapped by **Ravana**. Rama rescued her with the aid of the monkey **Hanuman**.

The lord Rama

Sita, Rama's wife

Lakshman, Rama's brother

Loyal helper and monkey, Hanuman

HANUMAN WORSHIPING RAMA

SITA

Sita was born from the earth and raised as King Janaka's daughter. **Rama** married her, then rejected her, because he suspected that she had been unfaithful with **Ravana**. When Sita undertook an ordeal by fire, **Agni** protected her. Although they were reunited, Rama was jealous and sent Sita into exile.

HANUMAN

Rama met the monkey king Sugriva, who had been dethroned by his half-brother Balin. Rama helped Sugriva win back his throne, and as a reward, Sugriva gave Rama an army of monkeys, led by Hanuman. Hanuman found where **Sita** was imprisoned, and went back to tell Rama. The monkeys built a bridge across the sea to Sri Lanka, and launched an assault on the palace. Rama finally defeated Ravana in single combat.

LAKSHMAN

King Dasharatha had four sons – **Rama**, **Bharata**, and the twins Shatrughna and Lakshman. The latter became Rama's loyal follower and accompanied Rama into battle against **Ravana**. In some stories, it was he, not Rama, who killed the demon king of the rakshasas.

RAVANA

The evil king Ravana ruled in Sri Lanka. The gods were so outraged by his cruel behavior to everyone that they sent **Rama** to earth as **Vishnu**'s seventh **avatar** to kill Ravana. Ravana kidnapped **Sita**, at the request of Shurpanakha, a female demon, who had tried, and failed, to seduce Rama. Ravana took Sita to his golden palace on Sri Lanka. Rama destroyed the palace, guarded by the rakshasas' army, in order to rescue Sita.

MANU

The first man, Manu was the son of **Brahma** and **Sarasvati**. Brahma took the form of a fish, telling Manu that the world would be destroyed by a flood and that he should build a large boat and put in it the seeds of all the living things on earth. As the flood waters rose, everything was submerged and Manu's boat was stranded on the Himalayas' highest peak. Eventually, the flood waters subsided. Manu made offerings that grew into a beautiful woman, Parsu. She and Manu became the parents of the human race.

Wheel of Life contains six realms into which people can be reborn

YAMA, GOD OF DEATH

YAMA

In some myths, Yama is said to be the first man, but he is also said to be the god of the dead and ruler of the underworld. His father Vivasvat, the sun, gave him this position. The Buddhist symbol of the Wheel of Life is depicted within the arms and jaws of Yama.

NAGAS

Pictured as cobras, nagas were dangerous, destructive serpents. Traditional enemies of the eagle **Garuda** (**Vishnu**'s steed), they were related because Kadru, their mother, was sister of Vinata, Garuda's mother. The chief naga was the serpent **Vasuki**, used by the gods to bring about the churning of the ocean.

Serpents were traditionally depicted as cobras

CHIEF NAGA VASUKI, A SERPENT WITH MANY HEADS

ASURAS

The asuras were demons – the traditional enemies of the Hindu gods. They helped the gods twist Mount Mandara in the churning of the ocean, to produce the elixir. The asuras fought the gods for the elixir, but the gods won, so only the gods became immortal.

THE GREAT GODDESS

HINDUISM HAS COUNTLESS GODDESSES, but many of them are regarded as aspects of Mahadevi, "the great goddess," sometimes called Devi, "the goddess." In early Indian cultures, Mahadevi was the mother goddess, one of the most important creative forces in the entire cosmos. She brought fertility to the earth, but also demanded that devotees make living sacrifices to her. Later the Hindu religion adopted Mahadevi as the wife of Shiva, a role in which she takes benign forms such as those of Sati and Parvati. In these incarnations, she is a loving, caring figure, but she can also take more fearsome forms such as Durga and Kali.

DEVI, "THE GODDESS," WIFE OF SHIVA

Devi is usually depicted with four arms

Dancing on a small animal figure

SHAKTI
Some Hindus believe that goddesses are aspects of Mahadevi. But others believe that feminine energy, or shakti, is the force from which goddesses were created. They believe that when the great triad of gods – **Brahma**, **Vishnu**, and **Shiva** – met, their glances created an energy that produced an essence of femininity so dazzling it lit up the heavens. This feminine shakti then divided into three goddesses – **Sarasvati**, **Lakshmi**, and **Parvati**.

DEVI
Some Hindus refer to Mahadevi as Devi, which means "the goddess." She appears in many different forms, often as the wife of **Shiva**. As Shiva's wife, her femininity is said to balance Shiva's masculine nature perfectly, and this balance leads to order and justice in the world.

Sati throwing herself onto a fire

SATI'S SUICIDE BY FIRE

SATI
Sati, one of Mahadevi's incarnations, was the daughter of the creator god Daksha. She was the ideal of feminine love and married **Shiva** against her father's wishes. When Daksha invited all the gods except Shiva to a special sacrifice, Sati was so angry that she killed herself. When Shiva danced a dance of death and destruction, **Vishnu** reincarnated Sati into **Parvati**.

DURGA IN COMBAT WITH THE DEMON KING, MAHISHA

Many-armed Mahisha was able to change shape

Durga thrusts her lance into the demon's heart

Durga rides on a lion

PARVATI AND SKANDA

PARVATI
As well as being a reincarnation of **Sati**, Parvati was said to be daughter of the mountain king, Himalaya. At first, **Shiva** did not notice Parvati, so Kama, the god of love, brought desire to the heart of Shiva by firing an arrow at Shiva while he was meditating. Shiva was captivated by Parvati, so they married and had a child, whom they named **Skanda** (Karttikeya).

DURGA
One of Mahadevi's more fearsome incarnations was Durga. As warrior goddess, she fought demons who brought peril to the world. On one occasion she defeated a demon, also called Durga, by turning herself into millions of soldiers to defeat his army and growing thousands of swords from her fingers.

KALI

Once Durga got so angry she produced another terrifying deity, Kali, who sprang roaring from her forehead. Kali had a black face, large fangs, a tongue like a flame, and a withered appearance. She wore a necklace made of human skulls and is often shown holding a severed head.

BENIGN KALI
Usually portrayed as a frightening, destructive figure, Kali has two other names – Chandi, the fierce, and Bhairavi, the terrible. Occasionally, however, she is shown in a less aggressive pose, with one hand raised in a blessing, a signal to her followers not to fear her.

BENIGN KALI

WRATHFUL KALI
Kali helped **Durga** defeat a demon called Raktabija, who could not be killed because he could produce another demon from each drop of his shed blood. Kali lapped up the blood, gobbled up the new demons, and defeated Raktabija. Drunk on blood, she danced a dance of death.

Cobra

Sword for cutting off demons' heads

Kali is sometimes shown with more than two arms

Matted hair

Severed head is a symbol of death

Garland of skulls – a symbol of reincarnation

WRATHFUL KALI

LAKSHMI
The wife of **Vishnu**, Lakshmi is goddess of good fortune and giver of wealth. One account of her birth says she appeared fully formed, carrying a lotus in her hand, during the churning of the sea of milk. She was reborn for each of Vishnu's incarnations. A goddess of perfect beauty, Lakshmi is usually portrayed with two arms, although it was sometimes said she had four.

RADHA
A young cowherd or milkmaid, Radha grew up in the tribe with whom **Vishnu** was raised. The two fell in love, and their devotion reflects the adoration that all worshipers feel for **Krishna**.

LAKSHMI, VISHNU'S WIFE

SARASVATI, GODDESS OF POETRY, MUSIC, LEARNING, AND SCIENCE

GANGA
The goddess Ganga represents the Ganges, India's holiest river, and purifies those who bathe in her. **Shiva** gave her six tributaries, so that she would not cause damage by flooding.

USHAS
Dawn goddess Ushas, daughter of heaven and sister of night, was worshiped as the link between heaven and earth. She was reborn every morning, when she rode across the sky in her chariot drawn by seven cows.

ADITI
Hindus worshiped Aditi as the mother of the gods and of the sun, moon, night, and day. She was an all-sustaining, life-giving force, who had 12 children – one for each month of the year.

Lotus flower

SARASVATI
The wife of **Brahma**, Sarasvati was given the power to create whatever Brahma dreamed up in his head. She became the goddess of the creative arts and of language. She invented Sanskrit, the language of the Hindu scriptures, and receives all words as the ocean receives all streams.

CHINA AND JAPAN

China has one of the world's oldest civilizations. By c.1500 BC, metalworking and writing had both developed, and Chinese mythology, with its creative heroes and deified ancestors, was well established. Japan has its own mythology, and its own religion, Shinto.

THE GODS OF CHINA

The earliest Chinese deities were nature spirits or spirits of people who once lived on earth. A pantheon evolved, to mirror the Chinese state of emperors, generals, sages, and a vast heavenly civil service. Over many centuries, the Chinese added to their mythology. Under the influence of Taoism, a new group of gods entered Chinese temples, and Buddhism, imported from India, introduced additional stories into Chinese mythology.

BODHISATTVA, A BUDDHIST SAINT

THE MYTHS OF JAPAN

Japan's most important deity, the sun goddess Amaterasu, was said to be the emperor's ancestor and a symbol of the "Land of the Rising Sun." There are many other Shinto deities, from storm gods to demons and underworld gods. Buddhism had a strong influence, and some Shinto gods are incarnations of Buddha.

SPELLING SYSTEMS FOR CHINESE NAMES

Chinese characters can be transcribed using the Wade-Giles or Pinyin systems. This book uses the former. Pinyin is in parentheses.

MAJOR CHINESE GODS

OF THE THOUSANDS OF CHINESE GODS, only a few play a major role in the creation of the cosmos and the mythical worlds of heaven and the underworld. Their images are placed prominently in Chinese temples, alongside other lesser, but popular deities. Chinese people visit these temples whenever they have a particular problem or a specific wish, to contact the appropriate god or goddess. For example, if they are worried about drought, they will make an offering to one of the gods of rivers and lakes. The stories of these deities involve the mixture of Buddhist, Confucian, and Taoist faiths that gives Chinese religion its special flavor.

Nū WA AND FU HSI

YIN AND YANG

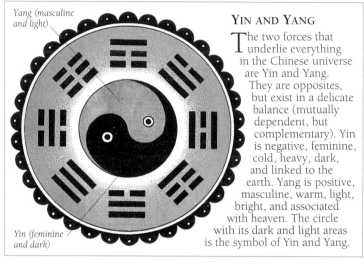

Yang (masculine and light)

Yin (feminine and dark)

The two forces that underlie everything in the Chinese universe are Yin and Yang. They are opposites, but exist in a delicate balance (mutually dependent, but complementary). Yin is negative, feminine, cold, heavy, dark, and linked to the earth. Yang is positive, masculine, warm, light, bright, and associated with heaven. The circle with its dark and light areas is the symbol of Yin and Yang.

NŪ WA

The creator goddess Nū Wa was also a fertility deity. Long ago there was a great flood, and the only survivors were Nū Wa and her consort **Fu Hsi**. When the flood subsided, they turned into a pair of snakes with human heads. They mated, and their children became the plants and animals of the world. In another version of the myth, Nū Wa formed new people out of balls of mud.

FU HSI

The emperor Fu Hsi (Fu Xi) was said to be the founder of China. He was the first ruler, established the first laws (especially those of marriage), devised clan and family names, and worked out the first calendar. He was a great inventor and showed people how to work metals, made the first musical instruments, and created the first Chinese script.

YI

Known as the excellent archer, Yi (I) is an ancient Chinese hero. It was said that long ago there were ten suns in the sky, and these suns made it too hot and scorched the earth. Yi shot nine of them down with his bow and arrows, which left only one sun.

CREATOR GOD EMERGING FROM COSMIC EGG

Pan Ku

CHANG-O AS A TOAD

PAN KU

Yin and **Yang** were contained inside a gigantic egg. As the two forces strove against each other, they broke the egg in two, revealing the creator god Pan Ku (Pan Gu). As the god emerged, the earth and sky moved away and Pan Ku, in the middle, kept them apart. For 18,000 years, the god worked on the creation, chipping away with his hammer and chisel, helped only by a dragon, a phoenix, a unicorn, a tiger, and a tortoise. When he died, his breath became the wind, his eyes the sun and moon.

CHANG-O

The wife of the hero **Yi** was Chang-o (Zhang O). In a famous myth about the couple, Yi finds the priceless elixir of life. Chang-o steals the elixir, drinks it, and floats to the moon to become the moon goddess, but she turns into a toad on the way. Yi is devastated.

HSI WANG-MU

Known as Queen Mother Wang, Hsi Wang-mu (Xi Wangmu) – the queen of the heavens and **Yü Huang Shang-ti**'s wife – lived in a palace built entirely of jade. She was the patron of women, and people prayed to her when a daughter was born. It was Hsi Wang-mu who gave the elixir of immortality to **Yi**.

KUN L'UN MOUNTAIN

The Chinese paradise was at the center of the earth, at the top of a mountain called Kun L'un. This was the home of the gods, and the location of **Hsi Wang-mu**'s palace and her garden.

PEACHES OF IMMORTALITY

In **Hsi Wang-mu**'s garden grew a peach tree, whose fruit made the eater immortal. **Sun Wu-k'ung** (Sun Wukong) went to heaven and stole the peaches. All heaven's gods and officials fought with him to retrieve the peaches before he was captured by the Buddha.

QUEEN MOTHER WANG

YÜ HUANG SHANG-TI

SUN WU-K'UNG

The adventures of the Monkey King, Sun Wu-k'ung, are told in the famous Chinese novel *Journey to the West*. After he was caught stealing peaches from **Hsi Wang-mu**'s garden, the kindly goddess of mercy, **Kuan Yin**, spoke up for him, and he was allowed to go to earth to escort Tang Seng, a Buddhist pilgrim, on a trip to India.

GOD OF HAPPINESS

YÜ HUANG SHANG-TI

The Jade Emperor – Yü Huang Shang-ti (Yü Huang Shangdi) – ruled the heavens. His kingdom was seen as a heavenly counterpart to the Chinese emperor's court on earth. Its ranks of civil servants received reports from all the household gods on the conduct of people on earth. He was probably an emperor on earth, who gave up his riches to help the sick before going to heaven.

THE THREE GODS OF HAPPINESS

Statues of the three gods of happiness are often seen in Chinese restaurants overseas. They stand for all the qualities Chinese people traditionally wish for. They are Fu Hsing – god of good fortune; Lu Hsing – god of wealth and high office (he was also a giver of sons); and Shou Hsing – god of long life (he was said to decide the dates when people died).

LUNG WANG

There were many dragon kings – or Lung Wang (Long Wang) – and they were gods of rivers, lakes, and the four oceans. Dragon kings represented wisdom, strength, and goodness. Protectors of ferrymen and water carriers, they were said to punish anyone who wasted water. They also brought rain, and offerings were made to them during droughts. When angry, the Lung Wang were said to bring fogs and earthquakes that damaged the river banks.

DRAGON, SYMBOL OF THE EMPEROR OF CHINA

Yin and Yang symbol

Paintbrush used to underline names of successful exam candidates

K'UEI HSING

The god of examinations, K'uei Hsing (Kui Xing) was most popular in Imperial times, when examinations were the important route to a job in the powerful civil service. He was usually portrayed as a man standing on the head of a sea creature such as a turtle. According to some stories, this was because he was originally a scholar who tried to commit suicide by throwing himself into the sea, but was rescued by a sea creature.

K'UEI HSING, GOD OF EXAMINATIONS

Bushel, used to weigh talents of exam candidates

Sea creature

YEN-LO WANG

There were 18 hells, distributed among ten law courts, which are presided over by the Yama kings. The supreme master of the world of hell and head of the first law court was called Yen-lo Wang (Yanluo Wang), who was just and lenient. He kept a detailed record of the good and bad deeds of people on earth, giving them fair sentences for wrongdoings and rewarding the good and repentant.

POPULAR CHINESE GODS

THOUSANDS OF MINOR DEITIES are still worshiped in Chinese temples. They may be Buddhist in origin, like the popular fertility goddess Kuan Yin, or Taoist figures, like the Eight Immortals. Household gods, gods of good fortune, patrons of particular trades or professions, and deities connected to the underworld all have their roles to play, especially when there is a problem relating to their area of interest. Their numbers are greater still because many of these gods have large numbers of followers who come to their aid on earth. Most of these gods were deified mortals – renowned emperors, sages, or ordinary people with remarkable achievements.

KUAN YIN

The goddess of mercy, Kuan Yin (Guan Yin), was a Buddhist deity originally from India. In China she is worshiped because she helped childless couples conceive and healed the sick. She is also a patron of travelers and farmers, and she protected souls in the underworld.

KUAN YIN, GODDESS OF MERCY

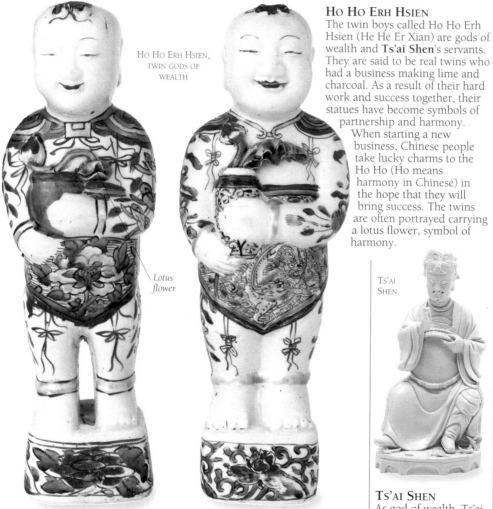

HO HO ERH HSIEN, TWIN GODS OF WEALTH

Lotus flower

HO HO ERH HSIEN

The twin boys called Ho Ho Erh Hsien (He He Er Xian) are gods of wealth and **Ts'ai Shen**'s servants. They are said to be real twins who had a business making lime and charcoal. As a result of their hard work and success together, their statues have become symbols of partnership and harmony. When starting a new business, Chinese people take lucky charms to the Ho Ho (Ho means harmony in Chinese) in the hope that they will bring success. The twins are often portrayed carrying a lotus flower, symbol of harmony.

THE EIGHT IMMORTALS

The Eight Immortals (Pa Hsien) were a group of Taoists who gained everlasting life. They flew through the air at fantastic speeds, and fought to banish evil from the world. They had many adventures. In one story, the immortals were returning drunk from a party, when Lan Ts'ai-ho was captured by the Dragon King's son, and a violent and bitter battle followed. The Eight Immortals are patrons of various groups: Chang Kuo-lao: the old; Lü Tung-pin: scholars; Chung-li Ch'uan: soldiers; Li T'ieh-kuai: the sick; Lan Ts'ai-ho: the poor; Ho Hsien-ku: unmarried girls; Hsiang-tzu: the cultured; and Ts'ao Kuo-chiu: nobility.

TS'AI SHEN

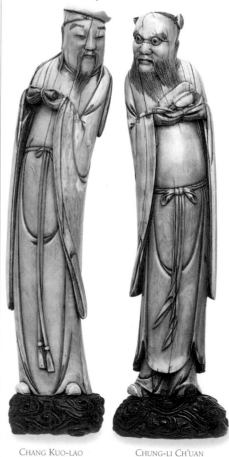

CHANG KUO-LAO CHUNG-LI CH'UAN

TS'AI SHEN

As god of wealth, Ts'ai Shen (Cai Shen) is very popular. People still pray daily to Ts'ai Shen, but the most important time to commemorate him is on the fifth day of the first month – his birthday. At New Year, people buy pictures and statues of him, last year's pictures are burned, and new ones are put in their place. Sacrifices such as a cockerel or a carp are made to Ts'ai Shen.

LU PAN

The god of builders, Lu Pan (Lu Ban) was head of public works in the heavenly civil service and patron of construction workers, from stone masons and woodworkers to decorators and plumbers. A great inventor, the mortal Lu Pan was the first boat builder and architect; he created umbrellas and wheelbarrows.

CH'ENG HUANG

The patron of fortified cities, Ch'eng Huang (Cheng Huang) is the god of walls and ditches, but his power stretches much farther than the city. As an underworld high official, he analyzes the lives of humans, and his reports calculate whether a person has lived his allotted number of days on earth.

TUNG-YÜEH TA-TI

The great emperor of the eastern peak, Tung-yüeh Ta-ti (Tong Yue Dadi) is god of the sacred T'ai Shan mountain and also the underworld's ruler. A most powerful god, he has ultimate power over when each human will die, and makes his calculations on an abacus. An abacus is often hung over his altar in temples.

HOUSEHOLD GODS

Many Chinese deities are worshiped in temples, but a few, like Kuan Yin and household gods such as Men Shen, are worshiped in people's homes. Plaques of deities, such as the hearth god Tsao Chün, are put up in the kitchen. At each year's end, offerings are made before the plaque; then it is burned, sending the god back up to heaven.

MEN SHEN

A pair of door gods, Men Shen, are often seen at temple entrances and also displayed by the front doors of houses. They are sometimes said to be deified heroes who killed evil spirits. The emperor was so pleased with their work that he ordered their statues to be placed at the gates of his palace, to ward off demons.

TSAO CHÜN

A plaque of the popular Chinese hearth god, Tsao Chün (Zao Jun) is placed near the stove in many Chinese homes. From here he can watch over the house. He delivers an annual report on each family member once a year to the gods of the Western Paradise. People sweeten his lips with honey so that Tsao Chün will only say good things about them.

Plaque to Tsao Chün

TSAO CHÜN WATCHES OVER
MEMBERS OF A CHINESE FAMILY

GODS OF MEDICINE

Historians of the Han dynasty (202 BC – AD 220) invented mythical emperors to explain the earliest period of Chinese history. First was **Fu Hsi** (Fu Xi), a patron of musicians, who invented musical instruments and the Chinese script. Next was Shen Nung (Shen Nong), god of agriculture and the first farmer. Last was Huang Ti (Huang Di), founder of civilization, who reigned for 100 years. All three of these deified emperors were expert in the healing properties of plants and are credited with inventing Chinese medicine.

Fu Hsi

Huang Ti

Shen Nung

SHOU LAO

The most important role of star god Shou Lao, which means "star of long life," was as the god of long life. Portrayed as an old, bald, smiling man, he usually carries a peach as a symbol of immortality, and may also hold a gourd, emblem of prosperity. He is attended by a group of animals – bats, cranes, and stags, the traditional Chinese symbols of happiness.

SHOU LAO, GOD
OF LONG LIFE

Peach, symbol of immortality

PAN K'OAN

In traditional Chinese belief, when people die their soul goes down to hell, where their actions on earth are investigated. In the law courts, the judge Pan K'oan decides how the soul should be punished. When all the sins are punished, the soul appears before a final judge, who decides how it will be reborn.

PAN K'OAN

Kuan Kung

Shou-ts'ang

KUAN KUNG

Kuan Kung (Guan Gong), also known as Kuan Ti or Kuan Yü, is a popular hero, to whom people pray for all kinds of protection. He was said to send his officer Shou-ts'ang to punish any wrongdoers. His strength was famous. One day, a butcher, Chang Fei, issued a challenge. His meat was stored in a well, covered by a 400-lb (180-kg) stone. Anyone who could lift the stone could keep the meat. Kuan Kung lifted the stone and was taking the meat when Chang Fei started to fight him for it. The hero **Liu Pei** stopped the fight, and the three became firm friends.

LIU PEI

Hero of a famous Chinese novel called *Romance of the Three Kingdoms*, Liu Pei led an army of volunteers to quell a rebellion and restore the rightful emperor to power. With his comrades **Kuan Kung** and Chang Fei, he was revered as an upholder of honor and duty. The trio are the Chinese equivalent of the Three Musketeers.

MAJOR GODS OF JAPAN

THE MYTHOLOGY OF SHINTO, the national religion of Japan, tells how the world was created by two primal deities – the god Izanagi and his consort Izanami, who lived on the High Plains of Heaven. This pair stood on the Floating Bridge of Heaven and gave substance to the cosmos, which they populated with a host of deities. They also created a group of islands, which became the islands of Japan itself. Their three most prominent children were the sun goddess Amaterasu, who was born from her father's left eye; the troublesome storm god Susanowo; and the moon god Tsuki-yomi. The eighth-century book the *Kojiki* tells of their many adventures, and shows the line of descent from the sun goddess Amaterasu to the human emperors of Japan. This divine ancestry meant that until the mid-20th century, the emperors of Japan were regarded as godly beings with a central role in Shinto religion.

EBISU, GOD OF FISHERMEN

IZANAGI AND IZANAMI

The creators Izanagi and Izanami stirred the ocean with a spear to make the first island. Here they built a house with a pillar, which they walked around in opposite directions. When they met, they joined in marriage. Izanami gave birth to the eight islands of Japan and many nature deities, such as **Kagutsuchi**, the fire god. When he burned Izanami, she died and became a vengeful deity in the underworld.

Izanami

Izanagi stirring the ocean with a spear

Amaterasu emerges from the cave

HIRUKO

The first child of **Izanagi** and **Izanami** was the deformed Hiruko, shaped like a gigantic leech. They felt such a monstrous offspring was unworthy. When they put Hiruko into a reed boat and set it adrift on the ocean, he became **Ebisu**, god of fishermen. This story may be the origin of an old Japanese custom, where parents mark the birth of the first child by placing a statuette in a reed boat and letting it float away.

KUNITOKOTACHI

The first living thing that arose out of the ocean of chaos was Kunitokotachi, the eternal land ruler, who grew in the shape of a reed. Out of Kunitokotachi were born seven generations of gods, the last being **Izanagi** and **Izanami**.

KAGUTSUCHI

Fire god Kagutsuchi burned his mother to death, so in revenge **Izanagi** cut off the fire god's head. Eight gods and goddesses were formed from the dead god's drops of blood, and eight mountain deities emerged from parts of his body.

SPIRITS OF YOMI

YOMI

When **Izanagi** went to Yomi (the underworld) to try to rescue **Izanami**, the spirits of Yomi attempted to kill him. Izanagi threw down his headdress, which turned into grapes, and his comb, which turned into bamboo shoots. Each time, the spirits stopped to eat. Izanagi escaped, blocking the entrance to Yomi with a boulder.

Uzume catching Raiden, the thunder god, in her bathtub

UZUME

The goddess of happiness was a dancing deity called Uzume. Her dance played a vital part in luring **Amaterasu** out of hiding.

AMATERASU

The sun goddess Amaterasu was so frightened by **Susanowo**'s violence that she shut herself away in a cave. Without the sun, the world was plunged into chaos and darkness, so the gods tried to entice her out. They lit bonfires, made the cocks crow, played music, and put a magic mirror outside the cave. The noise they made while **Uzume** was dancing made Amaterasu peep out. The gods told her that they had found a goddess who could shine even more brightly than the sun. As she looked at her own image in the magic mirror, the gods pulled her out of the cave, and sunshine was restored to the world.

Susanowo wreaking havoc

SUSANOWO

The storm god Susanowo did not want only to be ruler of the oceans, so he caused chaos on earth by destroying buildings, uprooting trees with his storms, and making hail and lightning from jewels given him by **Amaterasu**. Disgusted by his behavior, the gods expelled him from heaven, but he still wreaked havoc on earth.

TSUKI-YOMI

The Japanese moon god was Tsuki-yomi, who was made from drops of water that fell from **Izanagi**'s eye when the god washed himself after his trip to **Yomi**. Tsuki-yomi was **Amaterasu**'s husband, but they separated when Tsuki-yomi killed the rice goddess **Ukemochi**. Since then, night and day have always been separate.

NINIGI

Amaterasu's grandson Ninigi went to earth, where he defeated the bandit sons of the sorcerer-god Okuninushi and became ruler of the world. Ninigi took with him grains of the rice plant, and showed mortals how to grow these plants. Ninigi's descendants became the first mortal emperors of Japan.

WAKAHIRU-ME

The younger sister of **Amaterasu** was Wakahiru-Me, goddess of the rising sun. She was a companion of Amaterasu, who was also the goddess of weaving, responsible for the gods' clothes. **Susanowo** threw a flayed horse into the weaving room, terrifying the sisters and making Amaterasu hide in her cave.

TAKAMI-MUSUBI

This god was one of the oldest Japanese deities, born even before **Izanagi** and **Izanami**. Later he became messenger and principal assistant to **Amaterasu**. He sent her messages to and from the other deities, as well as bringing her information about what was happening on earth.

Oni

ONI

The demons known as Oni were said to live both on earth and in Jigoku, the Shinto hell. They could take human or animal shape, but were usually invisible. They used different disguises to create all sorts of misery on earth – disease, destruction, and famine. The Oni also stole souls or possessed the living, but were often thwarted by Shoki, the demon-queller.

Shoki the demon queller wrestles with two Oni

BENTEN

The goddess of music, good luck, and eloquence, Benten was wooed by the king of the serpents, who lived in the sea, terrifying the people of the coast and eating their children. Benten was put off by her lover's grisly reputation, but agreed to marry him if he would mend his ways.

HEROES

For hundreds of years, notable emperors, military leaders, statesmen, and other heroes have become Shinto gods. One of the most famous was the Emperor Ojin, who reigned during the fourth century AD, but was deified as Hachiman, the god of war, in the eighth century. There are still many shrines dedicated to deified heroes and heroines.

Kintaro

KINTARO

The Golden Boy Kintaro was possessed with supernatural strength. In one famous legend, he upturned a tree trunk and used it as a weapon to kill a giant spider.

Giant spider   *Upturned tree trunk*

RAIKO AND HIS FOLLOWERS KILLING THE GIANT SHUTEN-DOJI

RAIKO

Legendary warrior hero Raiko was famous for ridding the country of monsters, including the boy-faced giant, Shuten-doji (Drunken Boy), who drank human blood. Raiko disguised himself as a priest to get into the giant's stronghold, drug the attendants, and chop off his head.

Benten

King of the serpents wooing the goddess of music

INARI

The god Inari was married to the rice goddess **Ukemochi**. After **Tsuki-yomi** killed her, Inari took over her functions, to become god of the rice crop. An ancient patron of swordsmiths, he was also popular as a god of prosperity.

LESSER GODS OF JAPAN

THE PEOPLE OF ANCIENT JAPAN worshiped a multitude of minor divinities, whom they believed to be their ancestors. Gods inhabited every part of nature, from old gnarled pine trees and swift-flowing streams to soaring mountain peaks and jagged rocks. Even the stars in the heavens and the weather, particularly powerful storms, the wind, and thunder and lightning were granted godly status. Some of these deities guarded and protected the country of Japan. During the 13th century, when the emperor of China took to the seas to invade Japan, violent storms twice wrecked his fleet. This intervention by the heavenly powers became known to the Japanese as the kamikaze, or divine wind.

THE OLD MAN WHO MAKES THE CHERRY TREES BLOSSOM
According to one Japanese myth, every spring a mysterious old man appears and scatters ashes over the cherry trees to make them blossom. Flowering cherry trees have always had a special place in Japanese mythology and a beautiful tree is said to bring good luck. People flock to view the trees when the first blossoms appear.

OLD MAN WHO MAKES THE CHERRY TREES BLOSSOM

Bowl of ashes

Old man

SENGEN-SAMA

MOUNTAIN GODS
When creator god **Izanagi** cut the god of fire into five pieces, he created five mountain gods. They presided over different parts of the mountains, from the steep upper slopes to the mountain foot.

FUJIYAMA
Japan's mountains and volcanoes were often holy places. The most sacred of all was the dormant volcano Fujiyama (Everlasting Life). On its slopes are numerous shrines to different Shinto gods. Today, pilgrims wearing white robes climb the mountain to worship Sengen-Sama, the goddess of the rising sun.

STAR GODS
Various stars had godly roles. They could be good or evil, as shown by two of the most important – Amatsu-Mikaboshi, the god of evil, and Ama-no-Minaka-nushi-no-Kami, the Divine Lord of the Middle Heavens.

THE SEVEN GODS OF FORTUNE

A group of seven lesser gods – the Shichi Fukujin – represent happiness and good fortune. Only two of these deities, Ebisu and Daikoku, are Shinto in origin. The other gods are originally Buddhist from China and Hindu from India. Most of them have extra roles, representing qualities linked with happiness, such as prosperity or love.

HOTEI-OSHU

Large sack

BENZAITEN IN A BOAT WITH SOME OF THE OTHER GODS OF GOOD FORTUNE

BENZAITEN
Of Hindu origin, Benzaiten is a goddess of love, the equivalent of the Shinto goddess **Benten**. She rides a dragon and, like Benten, plays a biwa (a stringed instrument).

BISHOMONTEN
Bishomonten, god of war, comes from the Hindu pantheon. He is portrayed as a soldier who carries a lance and a miniature pagoda.

HOTEI-OSHU
Hotei-Oshu, the god of generosity and large families, came to Japan from Chinese Buddhism. He is depicted as a fat, bald-headed Buddhist monk, holding a large sack and a small screen.

FUKUROKUJU
The god of long life, Fukurokuju is of Chinese Buddhist origin. His high skull indicates that he is also a god of wisdom. A stork is his companion.

JUROJIN
Another god of long life from Chinese Buddhism, Jurojin is recognizable by his long staff. His usual companion is a stag.

Sack of rice

DAIKOKU

DAIKOKU
The Shinto god of wealth, Daikoku is surrounded by symbols of prosperity. He stands on two sacks of rice, with another sack on his back, and carries a hammer, also a sign of wealth.

EBISU
The Shinto god of work, Ebisu is a fisherman. He holds a large fish and a fishing line in his hands.

THE AINU

The original people of Japan – the Ainu – had their own myth of creation. The animals, gods, and demons lived in the upper and lower worlds, but in between was a vast bog in which earth and water were mixed. It was the task of the creator god, Kamui, to make something of this swamp.

KAMUI
The god Kamui created an enormous ocean resting on the backbone of a gigantic trout. He sent a bird to form areas of dry land by beating its wings and trampling the mud with its feet.

World's first squirrels

AIOINA
To show the Ainu how to hunt and cook their food, **Kamui** sent the god Aioina to earth. When he went back to heaven, the other gods complained that he smelled of human beings. The gods made Aioina take his smelly clothes back to earth. He left his garments on the ground, and his old sandals turned into the first squirrels.

Ball of thunder representing its sound

Thunder god depicted as a small demon

Drumstick to beat out the rolling thunder

THUNDER GODS
The Japanese had several thunder gods besides **Susanowo**. Take-Mikazuchi was conqueror of the province of Izumo, and Kami-Nari was known as the god of the rolling thunder. Trees that had been struck by lightning were sacred to Kami-Nari, and woodcutters were not allowed to chop them down.

JAPANESE GOD OF THUNDER

Jewel of the tides

RYUJIN

RYUJIN
The Dragon King of the Sea, Ryujin, was one of the most important Japanese sea deities, and can be recognized by his large mouth. Ryujin used his magic jewels to control the ebb and flow of the tides. When his daughter married Prince Hoori, she became an ancestor of Japan's royal family.

WATER GODS
The Kawa-no-Kami were river gods. When a river flooded, it was thought to be a signal for offering the god a sacrifice. There were also various sea deities, including the god O-Wata-Tsu-Mi. His subjects were the fish and sea creatures. The sea monster Wani was his messenger.

風神

WIND GODS
There were two principal wind deities in Japanese mythology. Wind god Shina-Tso-Hiko was created by the breath of **Izanagi**. Shina-to-Be was a goddess of the winds, and it was her special duty to blow away mist from the land.

Bag of winds

HOUSEHOLD GODS
The Shinto pantheon included several gods of the household. Most were kitchen gods, and included a popular deity called Kamado-no-Kami, the god of the kitchen range, who was worshiped all over Japan. The special god of the Imperial kitchen was a deified royal prince who had been a brilliant cook.

UKEMOCHI
Ukemochi was the goddess of food. On one occasion, when **Tsuki-yomi** went to see her, she produced an amazing meal by making rice and other dishes appear out of her nose, mouth, and rectum. Tsuki-yomi was so disgusted by the idea of a meal made in this way that he killed the goddess.

THE CLASSICAL WORLD

The people of ancient Greece and Rome had many gods and goddesses. These took human form and had loves and jealousies, friendships and quarrels,

just like humans. They also had a host of heroes, fantastic beasts, monsters, demi-gods, and other mythical beings.

FAMILIES OF GODS

Before the gods and goddesses were born, there was a generation of gigantic beings called the Titans. Two of these – Rhea and Kronos – were the parents of many of the deities. When the Romans conquered the Mediterranean world, the Greek stories of the parentage and exploits of the gods and goddesses proved so attractive to the Romans that they adopted them as their own, altering little except the deities' names.

KRONOS, FATHER OF MANY GREEK GODS

GREEK AND ROMAN NAMES

GREEK	ROMAN	GREEK	ROMAN
Aphrodite	Venus	Hephaestos	Vulcan
Apollo	Apollo	Hera	Juno
Ares	Mars	Hermes	Mercury
Artemis	Diana	Hestia	Vesta
Athene	Minerva	Poseidon	Neptune
Demeter	Ceres	Zeus	Jupiter

THE OLYMPIANS

THE MOST IMPORTANT GODS OF GREECE were those who lived on Mount Olympus and are often known as the Olympians. There were usually said to be 12 Olympians, plus Zeus, the most powerful god of all. When the gods were not busy with their own rivalries and loves (Zeus had many consorts, both divine and human), they often intervened in the lives of humans. For example, Athene protected heroes such as Herakles and Perseus, and helped to guide Odysseus home from Troy. But the influence of the gods was not always beneficial – it was the scheming of Aphrodite that led to the Trojan War.

Zeus driving his chariot

MOUNT OLYMPUS

After the gods and Titans clashed, the three most powerful gods divided up the cosmos – **Poseidon** ruled the sea, **Hades**, the underworld, and **Zeus**, the heavens. Zeus chose Mount Olympus to be his home, and there 12 of the principal gods and goddesses went to live with him. The weather was springlike, but a ring of ice separated the gods from the mortals below.

ZEUS

Youngest son of the Titans Kronos and Rhea, Zeus defeated the Titans in battle and became king of the gods. He was ruler of the gods who lived on **Mount Olympus** and upheld justice and social order. He punished his enemies with thunderbolts, made for him by the **Cyclopes**. In his special domain, the sky, Zeus fixed the order of the seasons and the courses of the stars. He had three wives – **Metis**, **Themis**, and **Hera** – and many affairs, with goddesses, nymphs, and human women.

ATHENE

ATHENE

Goddess of wisdom, Athene was born from **Zeus**'s forehead after he swallowed her mother **Metis**. Her symbol was the wisest of birds, the owl. Skilled in crafts such as weaving and the arts, Athene was also a warrior goddess who carried a spear – and a shield called the *aegis*, which bore the head of the gorgon **Medusa** and turned to stone anyone who saw it. Athene was patron of an area of Greece known as Attica, and its main city of Athens was named after her.

HERA

Zeus's third wife was Hera, goddess of marriage and childbirth, and queen of the Olympians. She was very jealous of her husband's affairs and wrought vengeance on her female rivals and their children. Her rivals included **Semele**, **Leto**, and Io, all of whom suffered as a result of Hera's jealousy. The Greeks called Hera's marriage with Zeus the Sacred Marriage, showing how important they felt the union between man and woman to be.

HERA, ZEUS'S THIRD WIFE

Cockerel

Many-breasted figure symbolizing Artemis as goddess of childbirth

APOLLO

The son of **Zeus** and the Titan **Leto**, Apollo was the god of light, the arts, medicine, and music. His light was the light of the sun, and – like the sun – he could be life-giving or destructive, benign or threatening. In his youth he was wild, and vengeful to any woman who spurned him. When **Cassandra** refused his advances, he gave her the gift of prophecy, but decreed that no one should believe her predictions. But eventually, he became calmer, using his gifts for healing, music, and foretelling the future through his oracle at Delphi.

APOLLO

ARTEMIS

Although **Apollo**'s twin sister Artemis, goddess of hunting, was often portrayed as a young woman with a bow, she also protected young animals. Artemis was chaste and she became angry if threatened. In the temple at Ephesus, a many-breasted statue also symbolized her as goddess of childbirth.

HERMES

The messenger of the gods, Hermes was the son of **Zeus** and the nymph **Maia**. As the god responsible for everything to do with movement, travel, roads, change, and commercial transactions, he was shown wearing a traveler's hat and winged sandals. In his hand he carried a magic wand made of two snakes coiled around a pole. Hermes had an unpleasant side – he sometimes carried lies and false reports, and he could preside over shady transactions, as well as fair deals.

Traveler's hat

Winged sandal

HERMES, MESSENGER OF THE GODS

DIONYSUS

God of wine and revelry, and son of **Zeus** and **Semele**, Dionysus could appear as a bull, a goat, or a youth. With the **Maenads** and the **satyrs**, he wandered the country, drinking wine and dancing wildly. Once captured by pirates, Dionysus escaped by turning the sea into wine and the pirates into porpoises.

ARES, GOD OF WAR

ARES

The terrifying Ares was the god of war. The son of **Zeus** and **Hera**, Ares was the incarnation of his mother's anger. Fearsome on the battlefield, with a war cry that could kill a mortal, he fathered several heroes who were almost as strong and terrifying as he. He was also the lover of **Aphrodite** and father of her child **Eros**. Aphrodite's husband, **Hephaestos**, was jealous of the affair, and trapped the pair in bed using a net so strong even Ares could not tear it.

Bull – one of Dionysus' many forms

DIONYSUS, GOD OF WINE AND REVELRY

Athene

Zeus

Hephaestos

HEPHAESTOS

The divine blacksmith Hephaestos was born so lame and so ugly that his mother **Hera** threw him into the Ocean River. Rescued by the nymphs, he became a famous craftsman, making beautiful ornaments from jewels and coral. Impressed by his talents, the gods brought him to Olympus and made him the god of fire and craftsmanship. His creations ranged from magic armor, which made the wearer invincible, to **Pandora**, the first woman.

Sea shell

APHRODITE, GODDESS OF LOVE

Eros, god of love

Trident used by Poseidon to sink entire islands or raise land from the seabed

POSEIDON, GOD OF THE SEA

APHRODITE

The name of the love goddess *Aphrodite* means "born from the foam" – she was said to have emerged from the sea. This most beautiful of goddesses could be cruel and capricious. She was married to **Hephaestos**, but her beauty captivated both gods and mortals. She had love affairs with **Ares**, **Hermes**, and **Dionysus**, and mortal men such as **Adonis**. Her children included the gods **Eros** and **Priapus**, and the hero **Aeneas**.

DEMETER

Goddess of crops and soil fertility, Demeter was worshiped together with her daughter **Persephone**. At Eleusis, near Athens, Demeter taught King Triptolemus how to plow his land and sow grain. Eleusis became famous for its secret rituals, which gave initiates the hope of a new life after death, symbolized by a head of grain, also an emblem of soil fertility.

DEMETER, GODDESS OF CROPS AND SOIL FERTILITY

POSEIDON

The sea god Poseidon was a powerful deity who, with a wave of his trident, caused thunderstorms and earthquakes. His anger was famous, and he quarreled with many of the other gods to try to gain power over different areas of Greece. His sacred animals were horses and bulls, which people sacrificed by throwing into the sea.

HESTIA

Goddess of the hearth and the eldest of the Olympians – which included **Poseidon**, **Demeter**, and **Zeus** – Hestia was the most peaceful of them all. She was a protector of family stability and social order, and presided over the naming of children.

LESSER GREEK GODS

THE ANCIENT GREEKS HAD MANY MORE GODS besides the Olympians. There was a host of lesser gods who filled a variety of roles. Some were deities who did not reach the high rank of the Olympians, while others were demigods or humans who were granted immortality. Many of them had a strong impact on everyday life on earth. These were the nature deities – such as the four winds, and the goddesses of the dawn, the moon, and the rainbow. Others were little more than abstract qualities, such as youth and justice. Still others were local gods and goddesses, who failed to gain popularity throughout all of Greece. But even these lesser figures could achieve fame. Asclepius, the god of medicine, for example, had a huge sanctuary at Epidauros in the Peloponnese, with temples, a stadium, and a vast theater, to which pilgrims flocked from all over Greece.

EROS, THE WINGED GOD OF LOVE AND DESIRE

PAN, GOD OF FIELDS AND WOODLANDS

GODS, TITANS, AND MORTALS

In one account of human creation, humanity appeared when an ancestor named Pelasgus appeared out of the soil. Another story tells how Zeus created a series of different races to occupy the earth – first came the good men of the Golden Age, next came the violent Silver Race, followed by the metalworkers of the Age of Bronze, then the Race of Heroes, and our own Age of Iron. Yet another myth tells how Prometheus shaped the first humans out of clay.

Prometheus

PROMETHEUS
The Titan Prometheus was a special protector of humanity. When **Zeus** and men met to share their food, Prometheus tricked Zeus into taking the bones and leaving the meat for the men. Zeus responded by taking fire away from earth. But Prometheus went to **Hephaestos**' forge and stole some fire for humans. He also taught people how to use fire to work metals.

PANDORA
In retaliation for the theft of fire, **Zeus** asked **Hephaestos** to make the first woman, Pandora, out of earth. Zeus sent her with a box to earth, where she married Epimetheus. Pandora wanted to see what was in the box, so she lifted the lid. All the ills of humankind escaped, and only hope was left inside when she replaced the lid. In another version of the story, the box contains blessings, but these escape back to heaven.

Human ills escaping

Pandora

PAN
With a human torso and the legs and horns of a goat, Pan, the son of **Hermes**, was the god of fields, shepherds, and woodlands. He enjoyed the company of **satyrs**, was a good dancer and musician, and liked chasing nymphs. Pan had a terrifying voice, which often startled animals in the woods. His shout could halt armies in their tracks and even fracture city walls – the fear it caused was the origin of the word "panic."

Cloven hoof

EROS
The winged child Eros was the embodiment of love. Some say he was born out of chaos at the beginning of time, others that he was the child of **Aphrodite** and **Ares**. His main role was to plague humans and even gods, carrying a torch to inflame their desires, or arrows that could pierce them with love.

PRIAPUS, GOD OF FERTILITY

PRIAPUS
The fertility god Priapus was **Aphrodite**'s son, and some said his father was **Hermes**, **Dionysus**, or **Zeus**. When the Trojan prince **Paris** chose Aphrodite as the most beautiful of the goddesses, she was pregnant with Priapus. Resentful that Paris did not choose her, **Hera** used her magic to deform the baby in Aphrodite's womb, making him ugly and ill-tempered. The gods threw him down to earth, where he became **Pan**'s companion. He was so hampered by his own lust that he could hardly move.

ASCLEPIUS
Asclepius, the son of **Apollo**, was the god of medicine. When Asclepius was young, Apollo sent him to the **centaur Chiron**, who taught him the arts of healing. The goddess **Athene** also helped Asclepius, giving him the blood of the **Gorgon**, which could bring the dead back to life. **Zeus**, worried by this power, struck him with his thunderbolt.

HYGEIA
Asclepius' three daughters were the goddesses of health – Iaso, Panacea, and, most prominent, Hygeia, who was often worshiped alongside her father. There was also a temple to Hygeia at the great sanctuary of Asclepius at Epidauros, where people went to worship the god and be cured of their ills by the priests.

EOS
The goddess of dawn was called Eos. She was the daughter of the Titan Hyperion and his sister Theia. Eos was known as Rosy-fingered Dawn, because of the warm pink tint of the sky at daybreak. It was her task each day to open the gates of heaven to let out the chariot of the sun.

HELIOS
Eos' brother was Helios, the sun. Shown as a handsome young man, rays of light radiated from his head. He rode a chariot pulled by four horses. Every day he traveled across the sky from east to west. At night, he followed a route underground, back to the east before starting his journey once more.

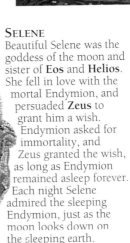

Selene

Endymion

SELENE
Beautiful Selene was the goddess of the moon and sister of **Eos** and **Helios**. She fell in love with the mortal Endymion, and persuaded **Zeus** to grant him a wish. Endymion asked for immortality, and Zeus granted the wish, as long as Endymion remained asleep forever. Each night Selene admired the sleeping Endymion, just as the moon looks down on the sleeping earth.

IRIS
Iris was the goddess of the rainbow, as well as a messenger of the gods. She was everhelpful, waiting on the gods and sometimes helping mortals who were in distress.

THEMIS, GODDESS OF JUSTICE

THEMIS
The Titan Themis was **Zeus's** second wife. On **Olympus** she was in charge of ceremonies and feasts, on earth the goddess of justice. She was known for her wise and fair advice, and even helped Zeus after he married his third wife, **Hera**.

THE FOUR WINDS
The four sons of **Eos** were Boreas, the savage North Wind; Notus, the warm, moist South Wind; Eurus, the East Wind; and Zephyrus, the favorable West Wind. The most famous wind was Boreas, who was worshiped by the Athenians because he blew away an invading Persian fleet. He abducted Oreithyia, daughter of Erechteus, king of Athens. They had several children, including the twins Zetes and Calais. When they died, the twins became northeasterly winds known as the Prodromes. Zephyrus was originally as savage as his brother, the North Wind, but he later mellowed, to become the gentle wind beloved by sailors.

The nymph Scylla

Glaucus tempted by Scylla

GLAUCUS
Originally a mortal, Glaucus achieved immortality by eating a magic herb. His fellow men refused to accept that he was immortal, so Glaucus took to the water and became a sea god. **Apollo** gave him the ability to foretell the future, so Glaucus would rise out of the sea to warn sailors of coming disasters.

PROTEUS
Known as one of the Old Men of the Sea, Proteus acted as the guardian of **Poseidon's** flock of seals. He had the ability to change into whatever shape he chose.

NEREUS
Like **Proteus**, Nereus was a shape-changing Old Man of the Sea. He lived with his wife Doris on the bottom of the sea. They had 50 beautiful daughters – the nereids.

HEBE
Hebe, the goddess of youth, was in charge of serving ambrosia and nectar, the gods' food and drink. The ideal servant, she helped **Ares** with his robes and **Hera** with her chariot. She found misfortune when **Zeus** made **Ganymede** his cupbearer. When **Herakles** was made immortal, Hebe became his wife.

THE ABDUCTION OF OREITHYIA BY BOREAS, THE NORTH WIND

LOVES OF THE GODS

MANY CLASSICAL MYTHS tell of the loves of the gods – both for each other and for human lovers. The most amorous of all the gods was Zeus, the king of the gods, who had numerous consorts. He often had to transform himself in order to take a human lover – both because he was too terrifying and dangerous in his true form and because his human consorts were often unwilling. The loves of the gods frequently caused confusion and misfortune, as when Metis was swallowed by Zeus, or Daphne was turned into a laurel tree. But they also enlarged the classical pantheon, bringing into existence a host of offspring, from the Fates to the Muses, many of whom had a profound influence on the lives of people on earth.

Leda taking pity on the swan

ACTAEON
Actaeon was brought up by a centaur called **Chiron**, who taught the young man how to become a skilled hunter. One day Actaeon was hunting when he caught sight of the goddess **Artemis**, herself a hunter, bathing in a river, and was stunned by the sight of the beautiful moon goddess. Artemis was known for her chastity and guarded it jealously. Outraged that Actaeon had seen her naked, she turned him into a stag, to be chased by his own hounds, who tore him to pieces.

Artemis turning Actaeon into a stag

LEDA
Faithful wife of King Tyndareus of Sparta, Leda was seen one day by **Zeus** when she was bathing in a river. Zeus plotted with **Aphrodite**, goddess of love, to seduce Leda. Aphrodite took the form of an eagle and Zeus turned himself into a swan. They flew past Leda, the eagle hunting the swan. Leda took pity on the swan, giving Zeus the chance to make love to her. Later, Leda produced two eggs. From the first hatched twin girls, **Clytemnestra** and **Helen**; from the second, the twin boys **Castor** and **Pollux**.

METIS
It was predicted that sea **nymph** Metis, first wife of **Zeus**, would have a daughter as wise as Zeus and a son who would seize his power. To prevent this, Zeus swallowed Metis, and her son was never born. But her daughter **Athene**, the goddess of wisdom, sprang, fully armed and perfectly formed, from the head of Zeus.

LETO
Zeus made love with Leto, making his wife **Hera** bitterly jealous. Hera banished Leto, who wandered the world, looking for a place to give birth. Since Hera's daughter, Eileithyia, goddess of childbirth, could not help Leto, the people of Delos let Leto give birth to the twins **Artemis** and **Apollo** on their island.

Zeus struggles with Ganymede

DANAE
When King Acrisius of Argos visited the oracle at Delphi, he was told that his daughter Danaë would have a son who would kill him. So Acrisius locked his daughter in a dungeon so that no man could find her. But **Zeus** found Danaë and came to her in a shower of gold. Danaë bore a son, **Perseus**. When her father discovered this, he pushed both Danaë and the child into a chest and threw them into the sea. However, Danaë and Perseus were washed ashore and returned to Argos.

Zeus visiting Danaë, locked in the dungeon

THE ABDUCTION OF GANYMEDE

GANYMEDE
The beautiful youth Ganymede was the youngest son of King Tros of Troy and his wife Queen Callirhoe. **Zeus** fell in love with Ganymede when he saw the boy looking after his father's flocks on the plain of Troy. Zeus turned himself into an eagle, flew to the Trojan plain, and abducted the youth. The god then took Ganymede to **Mount Olympus** and granted him immortality and everlasting youth. Ganymede also became cupbearer to the gods. Zeus gave compensation to King Tros for the abduction of his son, in the form of a golden vine made by **Hephaestos**, the god of fire and divine blacksmith. In another version of this myth, Zeus, rather than abducting Ganymede himself, sent an eagle to kidnap him. In either story Ganymede never saw his parents again.

PRINCESS EUROPA SITTING
ON THE BULL'S BACK

EUROPA

Zeus saw Princess Europa, daughter of the Phoenician king Agenor, when she was picking flowers in a field. When Zeus turned himself into a placid bull, the captivated princess sat on the creature's back. Suddenly, the bull ran into the sea and carried Europa away to the island of Crete. Here they had three sons: Minos (king of Crete), Rhadamanthus (a great lawgiver), and Sarpedon (king of Miletus).

DAPHNE

Eros, god of love, and **Apollo**, god of music and poetry, had a dispute when Apollo teased Eros about his skill in archery. Eros retaliated against his taunts by making him fall in love with Daphne, a beautiful **nymph** said to be the daughter of the Ladon River. Apollo chased the nymph and she ran toward the mountains. The god was catching up to her, so she begged her father to turn her into something else, to help her escape. Daphne was transformed into a laurel tree just as Apollo reached her. Her chastity was preserved, and ever since, the laurel has been Apollo's sacred tree.

DAPHNE AND
APOLLO

SEMELE

Zeus disguised himself as a mortal to have an affair with Semele, the daughter of Cadmus and Harmonia. **Hera**, Zeus's wife, took revenge. Disguised as Semele's old servant, Hera told Semele to ask her lover to appear in all his godly glory. At the sight of Zeus surrounded by thunder and lightning Semele was burned to death, but Zeus saved her unborn baby **Dionysus** from the flames.

SEMELE, LOVER
OF ZEUS

APHRODITE AND HER LOVER,
THE HUNTER ADONIS

MNEMOSYNE

The Titan Mnemosyne (Memory) was the daughter of Gaia, the earth, and Uranos, the sky. **Zeus** spent nine nights with her and Mnemosyne gave birth to the nine **Muses** – goddesses of the arts, astronomy, and history. A sacred spring was dedicated in Mnemosyne's memory at Lebadeia.

MAIA

Daughter of Atlas and Pleione, the **nymph** Maia was one of the seven Pleiades. She lived on Mount Cyllene, where she and **Zeus** had the affair that produced **Hermes**, the messenger of the gods. He was the only one of Zeus's illegitimate children not spurned by his wife **Hera**

ADONIS

Adonis was the son of the Assyrian king Theias and his daughter Myrrha. The gods transformed Myrrha into a myrrh tree to protect her from punishment for her affair with her father, and Adonis was born from the tree. Goddess of love, **Aphrodite** fell for Adonis as soon as she saw him, and decided that he should become her lover. She gave him to **Persephone** to guard, but she too fell in love with him and would not give him back to Aphrodite. Then **Zeus** intervened, ordering the boy to spend one-third of the year with Aphrodite, one-third with Persephone. He was allowed to choose for himself with which goddess he would spend the remaining third.

ARIADNE

Daughter of King Minos of Crete, Ariadne fell in love with the hero **Theseus**. She told him how to escape from the Cretan Labyrinth, where he went to kill the **Minotaur**. When Theseus left Crete, Ariadne sailed with him, but the god **Dionysus** fell in love with her, and cast a spell that made Theseus desert her on the island of Naxos. Dioynsus gave Ariadne a crown of seven stars, and when she died this became the Corona Borealis.

DIONYSUS FELL IN
LOVE WITH ARIADNE

Eros,
the winged
god of love

THEMIS

Daughter of Gaia and Uranos, Themis was the second of **Zeus**'s wives. She gave birth to many goddesses, including the three **Horai** – Dike, Eirene, and Eunomia – and their sisters the **Fates**, or Moirai. In some tales Themis was the mother of **Prometheus**, by her fellow Titan Iapetus.

COMPANIONS OF THE GODS

THE GODS OF GREECE AND ROME were accompanied on their travels by many supernatural creatures, who acted as servants, teachers, helpers, and followers. Each deity had his or her own retinue of followers, whose characters reflected the personality of the god. The drunken Dionysus, for example, was surrounded by an odd collection of mythical beasts and frantic dancing women, whereas the love goddess Aphrodite's companions were the beautiful Graces. Many of the gods' attendants played other roles, as spirits of specific places, or as deities with special responsibilities. Many were nature spirits, and to the Ancient Greeks and Romans they must have seemed closer to everyday life than the mighty gods of Mount Olympus.

FURIES

The Eurinyes (Raging Ones, or Three Furies) lived deep in Hades, where they tortured wrongdoers' souls. They were born from the drops of blood that fell on Gaia, the earth, when the god Uranos was castrated. Hideous to look at, with bodies of old women, heads of dogs, snakes for hair, jet-black skin, and bats' wings, their names reflected their grisly work: Tisiphone (Punishment), Megaera (Jealous Rage), and Allecto (Endless).

THE THREE FURIES

NYMPHS

Nymphs usually had one divine parent. Portrayed as beautiful women, nymphs were associated with the countryside, and there were several types: nereids and oceanids (nymphs of the seas), naiads (who lived in springs and streams), leimoniads (meadow nymphs), oreads (dwellers in the mountains), and dryads (nymphs of forests and woods). Many nymphs joined the retinues of the gods; **Pan** and the **satyrs** attracted a large following of nymphs, as did deities such as **Zeus**, **Apollo**, **Hermes**, and **Dionysus**. Only the dryads did not follow the gods, remaining in the forests to guard the trees and dance around sacred oaks. Most nymphs were Zeus's daughters; the main exceptions were the oceanids and the nereids (daughters of the Titan Ocean and the water god **Nereus**). Nymphs fell in love with human men.

THE OCEANIDS

CHIRON AND JASON

CHIRON

Unlike other **centaurs**, Chiron was always wise and kind. **Apollo** and **Artemis** taught him skills, such as medicine, music, and the arts of war. Chiron tutored the heroes **Achilles** and **Jason** in warfare and passed on his gift for healing to the god **Asclepius**. In **Herakles**' battle with the centaurs, Chiron was hit by a hero's arrow. He begged to die, because he knew that his wound would never heal.

PAN PIPES

ECHO AND NARCISSUS

SYRINX

The god **Pan** fell in love with the wood nymph Syrinx. When Pan chased her, Syrinx changed herself into a reed, to hide among reeds on a river bank. As he listened, Pan heard the sound of the wind sighing in the reeds, and had the idea of making a musical instrument out of reeds of different lengths. He called his instrument the syrinx, after the nymph he loved, but today it is more widely known as the Pan pipes.

ECHO AND NARCISSUS

The **nymph** Echo was a follower of **Zeus**'s wife **Hera**, whom she angered by endlessly talking about Zeus's love affairs. To punish her, Hera took away Echo's voice, so that she could only repeat what others said to her. Echo fell in love with handsome Narcissus, but she could not tell him. Vain Narcissus would only stare at his own beautiful reflection. Echo pined away among the rocks, leaving only her repeating voice behind.

Echo watches as Narcissus stares at his own reflection

Eros

GRACES

The Three Graces (or Charities) were the daughters of **Zeus** and the sea **nymph** Eurynome. Beauty personified, these elegant young women acted as **Aphrodite**'s handmaidens. Associated with spring, there were three: Aglaia (Shining), Euphrosyne (Cheerful), and Thalia (Bringer of Blossoms).

THE THREE FATES

FATES

The Fates (or Moirai), daughters of **Zeus** and the Titan **Themis**, controlled human destiny. The Fates were often portrayed as a trio of old women who sat spinning a thread – the thread of life. Their names were Clotho (who spun the thread), Lachesis (who measured its length and wound it up), and Atropos (who cut it).

THE THREE GRACES

Shining Aglaia

Cheerful Euphrosyne

Thalia, Bringer of Blossoms

Satyr, a wedding guest

Hora

Hora strewing flowers at wedding, to promote fertility and good fortune

THE MARRIAGE OF CUPID AND PSYCHE

HORAI

Sisters of the **Fates**, the three Horai – Eunomia (Discipline), Dike (Justice), and Eirene (Peace) – were goddesses of fairness and order who kept society under control. As nature deities, they looked after the budding, flowering, and fruiting of plants. Followers of deities such as **Aphrodite** and **Persephone**, they were close to **Hera** and looked after her horses and chariot.

SATYRS

Part-man, part-goat, satyrs were spirits of woods and mountains. As followers of **Dionysus**, they loved drinking and reveling, chasing **nymphs**, and frightening visitors to their forests. Satyrs were children of nymphs and goats. Originally human, they were transformed into their hybrid shape by the goddess **Hera**, who was angry that they did not guard Dionysus properly.

MUSES

Daughters of **Zeus** and **Mnemosyne**, the Muses were originally deities associated with mountains and springs. Later they became goddesses of the arts and followers of **Apollo**, who was given the title Apollo Musagetes (Leader of the Muses). The Muses lived on Mount Helicon in Boeotia near a spring called Hippocrene. There were nine in all: Calliope (Muse of Epic Poetry), Clio (Muse of History), Erato (Muse of Lyric Poetry), Euterpe (Muse of Instrumental Music), Melpomene (Muse of Tragedy), Polyhymnia (Muse of Mime), Terpsichore (Muse of Dancing), Thalia (Muse of Comedy), and Urania (Muse of Astronomy).

THE NINE MUSES NEAR THE SPRING OF HIPPOCRENE

SILENUS OFFERING A SACRIFICE AT A BLAZING ALTAR

SILENUS

The old man Silenus was a faithful follower of **Dionysus**. Fat, ugly, and a drunk, Silenus was very wise and passed on much wisdom to Dionysus. He followed Dionysus' procession, but was usually too drunk to walk. Either he was helped along by some **satyrs** or rode on an ass. His namesakes, the sileni, were satyrlike beings.

MAENADS

Dionysus' female companions were called Maenads (Mad Women). They dressed in flimsy costumes, played loud music, and took part in frantic dances. With an ability to tame wild animals, they rode on panthers and picked up wolf cubs in their hands.

GREEK HEROES

GREEK HEROES are usually the children of a god and a mortal. They are, therefore, stronger and braver than ordinary people. The tales of the heroes are some of the most exciting and violent stories in classical mythology. Many follow a similar pattern. The hero is often a prince who is deprived of his birthright by a jealous relative. He grows up in an alien country and has a number of adventures, often killing monsters or criminals and showing great bravery in battle. Finally, he returns home and rules his rightful kingdom.

PERSEUS AND MEDUSA

Perseus boasted that he could behead the **Gorgon Medusa**. But the Gorgon could turn a person to stone with one glance, so Perseus asked the gods for help. **Hermes** gave Perseus winged sandals; **Hades** lent his invisible helmet; and **Athene** gave him her polished shield. Perseus flew to the Gorgon's home with the winged sandals, and used the helmet to trick the **Graeae** who guarded the Gorgon's cave. He used Athene's shield as a mirror, so that he did not have to look directly at Medusa.

PERSEUS HOLDING MEDUSA'S HEAD

THESEUS

Son of Aegeus, king of Athens, Theseus slew the Minotaur, the monster that lived on Crete, and killed murderers and robbers such as Cercyon and Sciron. He fought with Herakles against the Amazons, defeated the efforts of the sorceress Medea to kill him, and became king of Athens.

Theseus

Sinus

THE BATTLE OF GOOD VERSUS EVIL

THESEUS AND SINIS

Poseidon's son, Sinis, was very strong. He would stop passers-by, torture and rob them, then pull them apart between two bent trees or use a bent pine to catapult them through the air. Theseus killed Sinis by hurling him over a cliff.

THESEUS AND THE MINOTAUR

THESEUS AND THE MINOTAUR

Every year King Minos of Crete demanded seven youths and seven maidens from Athens to feed to the monstrous **Minotaur** he kept in the labyrinth near his palace. When Theseus came from Athens to kill the Minotaur, **Ariadne**, Minos's daughter, said she would help him if he would take her away from Crete. She gave Theseus a thread to unwind so he could kill the beast and find his way out of the labyrinth. They escaped by ship, but stopped at Naxos. Here, **Dionysus**, in love with Ariadne, cast a spell so that Theseus forgot her and sailed away alone.

JASON

A prince of Thessaly, Jason was robbed of his throne by his uncle Pelias. To keep Jason away, Pelias sent him on an impossible mission – to capture the Golden Fleece, which was kept by King Aeëtes, in Colchis, by the Black Sea.

BUILDING JASON'S SHIP, THE *ARGO*

JASON AND THE ARGONAUTS

The hero Jason set sail in his ship, the *Argo*, which was built by the craftsman Argus. Jason's 50 traveling companions, called the Argonauts, included many Greek heroes. Their exciting adventures included clearing the terrifying giants from the land of Cyzicus, banishing the **Harpies** from the mouth of the Black Sea, and sailing through the Symplegades, two treacherous moving rocks.

JASON ESCAPES WITH THE FLEECE

JASON AND THE GOLDEN FLEECE

When Jason and the Argonauts arrived at Colchis, King Aeëtes did not want to part with the Golden Fleece. He gave Jason many impossible tasks to do before he could take his prize. With the help of the magic of the sorceress Medea, Aeëtes' daughter, Jason was able to grab the fleece and escape.

HERAKLES

The most famous Greek hero was Herakles (Roman Hercules). His bravery and strength were unique, but he also had an uncontrollable temper. He was the only human to be given immortality. His most famous deeds were the Twelve Labors set for him by Eurystheus, king of Tiryns, as penance for killing his wife and children.

GODLIKE STRENGTH

Zeus's wife **Hera** was jealous of his affair with the mortal Alkmene, who gave birth to **Herakles**. So Hera put two great snakes in Herakles' crib, hoping they would crush him to death. But the child used his superhuman strength and strangled the snakes.

THE INFANT HERAKLES KILLS THE GIANT SNAKES

THE TWELVE LABORS

1 NEMEAN LION
At Nemea there lived a lion with a skin so tough no weapon could pierce it. Herakles made a massive club, beat the lion, and strangled it. He used the beast's sharp claws to skin it and wore the hide for his protection.

2 LERNEAN HYDRA
The Hydra of Lerna was a nine-headed dragon. When one head was cut off, two more grew in its place. Herakles was helped by his nephew Iolaus,who burned each neck as soon as Herakles cut off the heads, so new heads would not grow.

HERAKLES AND THE NEMEAN LION

3 KERYNEIAN HIND
On Mount Keryneia lived a hind with golden horns – a creature sacred to the goddess **Artemis**. Herakles was asked to capture the hind, but not to harm it. He chased it for a year, finally catching it with a net, but the hind was wounded. Herakles blamed Eurystheus, so that Artemis would not be angry with him.

Herakles catches the hind

KERYNEIAN HIND

4 ERYMANTHIAN BOAR
This giant creature terrorized the people around Mount Erymanthus. Herakles had to bring the boar back alive to Eurystheus, who was so terrified by the beast that he hid in an urn.

Herakles brings the Erymanthian Boar to King Eurystheus

King Eurystheus of Tiryns hides from the boar in an urn

5 AUGEAN STABLES
Herakles cleaned years of accumulated dung from Augeas' stables, by diverting two rivers to wash away the filth.

6 STYMPHALIAN BIRDS
Man-eating birds preyed on people by Lake Stymphalos. Herakles frightened the birds out of the trees and shot them with his arrows.

7 CRETAN BULL
A fire-breathing bull (**Minotaur**'s father) rampaged across the island of Crete. Herakles had to catch the bull and take it alive to Tiryns.

8 MARES OF DIOMEDES
Thracian king Diomedes fed his mares human flesh. Herakles killed him and fed him to the mares. He tamed and took them to Tiryns.

9 GIRDLE OF HIPPOLYTE
Amazonian queen Hippolyte had a beautiful girdle that Eurystheus wanted. Herakles fought and killed the queen, and took the girdle.

10 CATTLE OF GERYON
Three-bodied monster Geryon kept a herd of red cattle. Herakles killed Geryon, his giant herdsman, and his hound, and captured the cattle.

11 APPLES OF THE HESPERIDES
Nymphs called the Hesperides had a tree bearing golden apples. It was guarded by Ladon, a dragon that Herakles had to kill to get the fruit.

12 CERBERUS
Herakles' final task was to capture **Cerberus**, the three-headed dog who guarded the entrance to the underworld, and take it to Tiryns.

DAEDALUS AND ICARUS
The artist, craftsman, and inventor Daedalus worked on Crete. He built the labyrinth for King Minos, but the king was so angry when **Theseus** killed the **Minotaur** and escaped that he imprisoned Daedalus and his son Icarus there. Daedalus planned an ingenious way out. He made wings for himself and Icarus, and stuck them on with wax. The two flew away from the island, and eventually Daedalus landed safely. But Icarus, in spite of his father's warnings, flew too near the sun. The wax melted, and he plunged to his death in the sea.

BELLEROPHON
The hero Bellerophon tamed the winged horse, **Pegasus**, killed the **Chimera**, and defeated armies, giants, and Amazons. Riding Pegasus, he soared toward **Olympus**, but he flew too high, fell to earth, and lost his eyesight when he fell into a thorn bush.

MYTHICAL CREATURES

GREEK MYTHOLOGY is full of stories about the marriages and couplings of many creatures. Some of these unions produced hybrid beasts or monsters, who were often hideous to look at and greedy for human flesh. These mythical monsters were usually terrifying, and were sometimes used by the gods to punish their enemies or attack people who made them angry. Often it was left to one of the great heroes, such as Perseus or Herakles, to kill these beasts or take away their power.

Triton

Sea nymph, or nereid

CYCLOPS

Single eye

CYCLOPES
The Cyclopes were giants, each with a single round eye in their foreheads. The first three were the sons of Gaia and Uranos. Imprisoned in the underworld, they were freed by **Zeus** and helped him fight their Titan captors. As Zeus's royal blacksmiths, they made his thunderbolts as well as **Poseidon**'s helmet.

HUNDRED-HANDED GIANTS
The Hundred-handed Giants (Hekatonchires) each had 100 arms and 50 heads. Three in number, they were the sons of Gaia and Uranos. Like their brothers, the **Cyclopes**, they supported **Zeus** when he waged his war with the Titans.

Eagle's head

JUG IN THE FORM OF A GRIFFON

GRIFFON
A griffon, with a lion's body and an eagle's wings and head, acted as a guardian for the gods, to watch over **Apollo**'s treasures and **Dionysus**' bowl of wine. In one myth, griffons lived in northern India, where they scared away gold diggers because they did not want their nests disturbed.

TRITON
The sea god **Poseidon** and his queen Amphitrite had a son called Triton, who was half man and half fish. Like his father, Triton had power over the waves. During a battle between the gods and the Titans, he terrified the Titans by the sound of his blowing into his conch shell. He could also be helpful – he saved the Argonauts when their ship was storm-bound. Triton gave his name to a whole race of scaly sea monsters.

CENTAURS
These wild creatures had the heads and upper torsos of men, but were horses from the waist down. Their characters were as mixed as their bodies. Centaurs were usually gentle and wise, their skills ranging from music to medicine. They could also be warlike, fighting many famous battles, including one with the Lapiths, a people who tanned the skins of their horses. Heroes **Jason** and **Perseus** got much of their wisdom from the centaurs.

Centaur / *Lapith*

Victims about to be sacrificed to Minotaur

Minotaur

MINOTAUR
This human-eating monster was part bull and part man. It was born on Crete, where King Minos ordered his craftsman, **Daedalus**, to build a labyrinth, or maze, to imprison the beast. **Theseus** put the creature to death.

SEA SERPENT
Queen Cassiopeia claimed that she and her daughter Andromeda were more beautiful than the nereids, followers of **Poseidon**. The sea god sent a sea serpent to punish Cassiopeia for her boasting. Andromeda was chained to a rock as food for the beast, but was rescued by the hero **Perseus** just as the beast was about to strike.

Perseus / *Sea monster* / *Andromeda chained to rock*

HARPIES

Birds with women's heads and sharp talons, the Harpies lived on islands in the Aegean where they preyed on people's souls. The Thracian king Phineus displeased the gods, who sent Harpies to peck out his eyes and steal his food. When the Argonauts arrived in Thrace, they had the North Wind's sons chase away the Harpies.

TERRIFYING HARPIES PREYED ON CHILDREN

SNAKE-HAIRED MEDUSA

GRAEAE

The names of these three women, sisters of the **Gorgons**, summed up their characters: Pemphedro (Spiteful) Deion (Terrible), and Enyo (Warlike). They shared one tooth and one eye. **Perseus** stole their one eye to help him kill **Medusa**.

ECHIDNA

This snakelike monster was known as the "mother of all monsters." She lived with the giant, Typhon. Their children included some of the most terrifying creatures in classical mythology – the **Chimera**, the Hydra, **Cerberus**, and the **Sphinx**.

SPHINX

In Greek legend, the Sphinx was a creature sent to punish the people of Thebes, who had displeased the gods. The monster ate anyone who could not answer this riddle: "Which animal has at first four legs, then two legs, then three legs?" No one could solve the puzzle until **Oedipus** realized that the answer was a human – who crawls as a baby, walks on two legs as an adult, and walks with a stick in old age. When the Sphinx heard this answer, she threw herself to her death on some jagged rocks.

Woman's head

Bird's wings

Lion's body

GORGONS

With snakes instead of hair and bodies covered with scales, the Gorgons (Stheno, Euryale, and **Medusa**) were terrifying. Their gaze was so deadly it could turn anyone who looked into their eyes to stone. They lived in an underground cave, and were guarded by their sisters, the **Graeae**.

MEDUSA

The most famous of the **Gorgons**, Medusa, was the favorite of her father, the sea god Phorcys. He gave her powers to transform herself into a beautiful woman. In return, she sacrificed her immortality. In one story, **Athene** was so jealous of Medusa's beauty that she turned her hair into snakes.

Pegasus

Perseus

Medusa's head

CHIMERA

This fire-breathing monster was part goat, part lion, with the tail of a snake. It was the child of the monsters Typhon and **Echidna**. The Chimera was kept as an awesome pet by the king of Caria, but it escaped and settled on a mountain in Lycia. It ravaged the kingdom from here, until King Iobates of Lycia ordered Prince **Bellerophon** to kill it.

Serpent's head as a tail

Goat's head

Chimera could breathe fire

PEGASUS

When **Perseus** killed **Medusa**, the winged horse Pegasus sprang from her blood. Prince **Bellerophon** tamed this fantastic beast and took him to Lycia to kill the **Chimera**. When the prince rode up to Mount **Olympus**, **Zeus** sent a fly to sting Pegasus, who threw the prince off.

Body and head of a lion

UNDERWORLD AND PUNISHMENTS

THE GREEKS BELIEVED that when a person died, his or her soul went to the underworld, the dark realm of King Hades and his queen, Persephone. In the underworld, called Hades after its ruler, the deceased were tried by three judges: Rhadamanthus, Minos, and Aeacus. If they had lived an evil life, they might be punished. The underworld had its own geography. The early Greeks placed it beyond the Ocean River, which encircled the world. Later, they thought it was beneath the earth. It had rocks, caves, five rivers, two special areas called Erebos and Tartaros, where souls were punished, and the Elysian Fields, the home of the blameless dead.

ORPHEUS AND EURYDICE
The great musician Orpheus was heartbroken when his wife, the **nymph** Eurydice, died of a snake bite. To bring her back, he traveled to the underworld, enchanting guard-dog **Cerberus** with his lyre. **Persephone** and **Hades** said that Eurydice could follow Orpheus back to earth, but he must not look back at his wife before leaving the gates. He could not resist doing this, so Eurydice had to stay in the underworld.

CHARON CROSSING THE STYX RIVER TO THE UNDERWORLD

PERSEPHONE AND HADES ON THEIR THRONE

Queen Persephone

Cerberus

King Hades

CHARON
The dead had to cross the rivers Acheron or **Styx** to get to the underworld, with the help of Charon, who ferried them across. A bad-tempered old man, Charon insisted that everyone who traveled on his ferry had to pay a one obol coin. This is why the Greeks always put a coin in the mouths of their deceased.

ELYSIAN FIELDS
The earliest Greeks believed good people went to the Elysian Fields (or Elysium) after death. The fields lay on the far side of the Ocean River, which people thought encircled the earth. It was a beautiful place where dead souls enjoyed sports, poetry, and music. The ruler of the Elysian Fields was the Titan Kronos.

HECATE, GODDESS OF MAGIC

STYX AND OTHER RIVERS
The underworld had five rivers. The Acheron (Distress) was full of stagnant, bitter water, while the Phlegethon (Fire) contained liquid flames. The Cocytus (Wailing) was haunted by the unburied dead, who stayed there for 100 years. The longest, the Styx (Hateful), circled the underworld nine times. The dead drank the waters of Lethe (Forgetful) to forget their past lives.

HADES
God of the dead, Hades was the son of the Titans Kronos and Rhea. Although he was **Poseidon**'s and **Zeus**'s brother, Hades did not live on **Mount Olympus** but in the underworld, where he looked after the dead. Also god of wealth, Hades had rich mines under the earth, and was connected to the bounty of the fields through his marriage to **Persephone**, daughter of the corn goddess **Demeter**.

PERSEPHONE
Once when **Hades** was visiting earth he caught sight of the fertility goddess Persephone, carried her off in his chariot, and married her. She became ruler of the underworld with Hades. Persephone's mother **Demeter** was angry and threatened to stop the crops from growing if her daughter was not returned. **Zeus** agreed Persephone should spend two-thirds of her year on earth and one-third with Hades.

CERBERUS
Hades' three-headed dog, Cerberus, guarded the underworld. He was kept at the gate of the underworld, preventing the living from getting in and frightening the souls of the dead as they entered.

HECATE
The goddess Hecate, sorceress and patron of magicians and witches, lived in Hades where she presided over spells and ceremonies. She would come to earth with her hounds, and appear in various forms – as a she-wolf, a mare, or a woman with three bodies or heads. Often Hecate was seen at crossroads, where statues were erected to her.

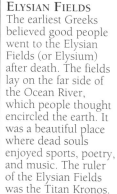

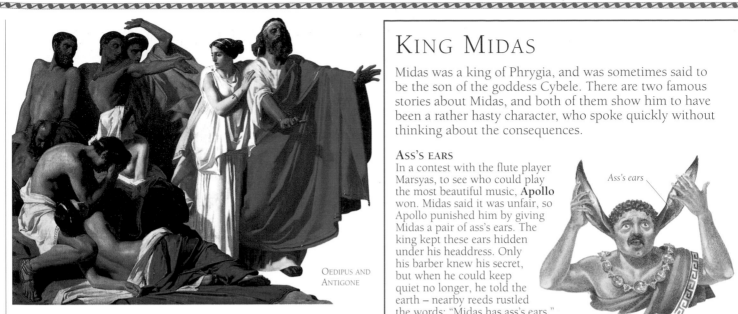

OEDIPUS AND
ANTIGONE

KING MIDAS

Midas was a king of Phrygia, and was sometimes said to be the son of the goddess Cybele. There are two famous stories about Midas, and both of them show him to have been a rather hasty character, who spoke quickly without thinking about the consequences.

ASS'S EARS

In a contest with the flute player Marsyas, to see who could play the most beautiful music, **Apollo** won. Midas said it was unfair, so Apollo punished him by giving Midas a pair of ass's ears. The king kept these ears hidden under his headdress. Only his barber knew his secret, but when he could keep quiet no longer, he told the earth – nearby reeds rustled the words: "Midas has ass's ears."

Ass's ears

OEDIPUS

When an oracle forecast that Oedipus would kill his father King Laius and marry his mother Queen Jocasta, Laius left Oedipus to die. But Oedipus was rescued and years later unknowingly killed Laius and married Jocasta. When Jocasta discovered who he was she killed herself. Oedipus blinded himself and went into exile with his daughters Antigone and Ismene.

Everything
Midas touches
turns to gold

TANTALUS

King Tantalus, ruler of Lydia (in modern Turkey), doubted that the gods were really all-powerful and all-knowing. He invited them to a banquet and served up Pelops, his son, to test whether they knew what they were eating. Right away, the gods realized what Tantalus had done. They brought Pelops back to life and sentenced Tantalus to everlasting thirst and hunger in Hades.

THE GOLDEN TOUCH

Peasants brought the drunken **satyr Silenus** in chains to Midas. Recognizing Silenus as **Dionysus'** companion, Midas returned him. As a reward, Dionysus granted Midas a wish. The wish (anything Midas touched turned to gold) was granted, but it failed – even his food and wine became gold. Begging for an end to his torment, Midas was told to wash in a river, where, ever since, grains of gold have been found.

Zeus

Eagle pecking at
Prometheus'
organs

SISYPHUS

King Sisyphus of Corinth did not want a funeral. This offended **Hades**, who sent him back to earth for burial, but Sisyphus went back to his throne. When he died, he was forced to roll a rock up a hill in the underworld, forever.

ZEUS
CHAINING
PROMETHEUS
TO ROCK

PROMETHEUS

The Titan Prometheus looked after humankind, often at the expense of the gods. He tricked **Zeus** into accepting bones to eat, reserving the flesh for humans. Then he stole fire from **Hephaestos**, taking it to earth and showing people how to use it to work metal. In anger, Zeus chained Prometheus to a rock and sent an eagle to peck out his liver. The torment continued, because each time the liver grew back, the bird pecked it out again.

TROJAN WAR

WHEN PARIS, THE PRINCE OF TROY, with the help of Aphrodite, stole Helen, the wife of King Menelaus of Sparta, a bitter, ten-year war between Greece and Troy began in Asia Minor (Turkey). The conflict involved many of the great Greek heroes, including Achilles, who had been dipped in the Styx River as a child, so that his whole body, except for his heel, was invulnerable. The Greeks were led by Agamemnon, brother of Menelaus and king of Argos. The Trojan leader was Hector. The gods were also involved – some of them backed Greece, others the Trojans. The entire story, ending in victory for the Greeks, was told by their poet Homer (c.850–800 BC) in his epic, the *Iliad*.

MENELAUS AND HELEN

Hera

Aphrodite

Paris

CLYTEMNESTRA AND AEGISTHUS WATCHING AGAMEMNON

PARIS
The goddess Eris (Strife) sent a golden apple to the wedding of Peleus and Thetis. It was marked "For the fairest." **Zeus** asked Paris, Prince of Troy, to choose which goddess should receive the apple. **Athene** promised Paris wisdom if he chose her, **Hera** offered power, but **Aphrodite** promised him the most beautiful woman in the world, and so it was she who received the apple.

AGAMEMNON
Agamemnon, King of Argos, led the Greeks against Troy, but he was beset with problems. When his fleet was becalmed, he was forced to sacrifice his daughter Iphigeneia to get a fair wind. In the Trojan War, Agamemnon fought bravely until he was wounded and had to withdraw from battle.

CLYTEMNESTRA
Agamemnon's wife was Clytemnestra, who came from Sparta. Bitter at the loss of her daughter Iphigenia, she took Prince Aegisthus as her lover while Agamemnon was away fighting at Troy. When Agamemnon returned, Clytemnestra threw a net over him as he stepped out of his bath, and Aegisthus stabbed him to death.

MENELAUS
King Menelaus ruled Sparta in southern Greece. When Menelaus was told of the abduction of his wife **Helen**, he called together all his Greek allies. But he was not a violent man. He asked for his wife's return, then fought **Paris** in single combat, before the war broke out.

HELEN
The queen of Sparta, Helen was famed for her beauty. She was **Paris**' prize for giving the apple to **Aphrodite**. Paris and Helen eloped to Troy when **Menelaus** was away at the funeral of his grandfather, Catreus, on Crete. Their flight caused the Trojan War to start.

ACHILLES AND PATROCLUS
The greatest Greek warrior was Achilles, who pulled out of the fighting in protest when **Agamemnon** claimed his war booty. Achilles' best friend Patroclus put on Achilles' armor, to make the Trojans think that Achilles had returned to the fight. A battle followed and Patroclus was killed. In despair, Achilles rejoined the battle, in which he killed the Trojan hero **Hector**. But then Achilles himself was fatally shot in the heel by **Paris**.

ACHILLES FINDS THE BODY OF PATROCLUS

ORESTES KILLS AEGISTHUS

ORESTES
Agamemnon's son Orestes was away when his mother **Clytemnestra** and her lover Aegisthus murdered his father, but he vowed to avenge the death. Years later he returned, entering the palace with his sister Elektra's help. His mother did not recognize him, and she and Aegisthus were put off guard believing him dead. Orestes killed Aegisthus before beheading Clytemnestra.

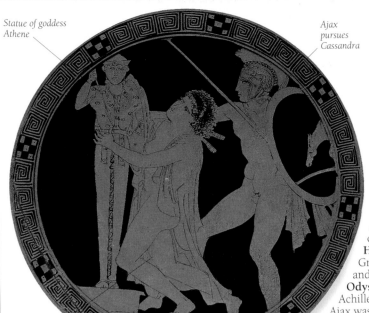

Statue of goddess Athene

Ajax pursues Cassandra

Cassandra

Trojans pulling the horse

TELAMONIAN AJAX

Another Ajax, son of King Telamon of Salamis, was given his strength by **Herakles**. One of the most heroic Greek warriors, he secured the body and armor of the dead **Achilles** while **Odysseus** held back the Trojans. When Achilles' armor was awarded to Odysseus, Ajax was jealous and decided to kill the Greek leaders. Instead, **Athene** made him mad, and he killed a flock of sheep. Later he committed suicide.

TROJAN HORSE

The Greeks made a hollow wooden horse and left it outside the walls of Troy, but 50 Greek warriors were hidden inside. The Trojans took the horse into the city, thinking it was a peace offering and the Greeks had gone home. At nightfall, the Greek warriors left the horse and opened the city gates so the Greek army could enter and defeat the Trojans.

CASSANDRA

As Troy burned, Ajax found **Priam**'s daughter Cassandra in **Athene**'s temple, clinging to her statue for protection. He tried to rape her, but Athene, borrowing **Zeus**'s thunderbolt, killed him. Cassandra could foretell the future, but no one would believe her prophecies. After the war, she went to Greece with **Agamemnon**. When she warned him of danger, he took no heed and was later murdered in his palace by his wife.

Hector

Andromache

Astyanax

THE FLIGHT FROM TROY

When the Greek army thundered through the gates of Troy, the gods told Aeneas and Anchises to round up some survivors, board a ship, and flee the city. They made a long journey across the Mediterranean, stopping in Sicily and at Carthage in North Africa before arriving in Rome to build a city even more magnificent than Troy.

ANCHISES

The cousin of Troy's King **Priam**, Anchises was so handsome that **Aphrodite** fell in love with him. **Aeneas**, who inherited the good looks of both his parents, was the child of their relationship.

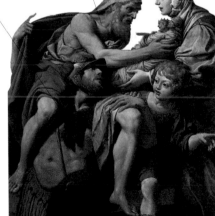

Anchises

Aeneas

ANDROMACHE

Hector's wife Andromache was the most long-suffering of the Trojan women. During the war she was raped, made a slave, and forced to hand her baby to the Greeks, who threw him over the city battlements. But she bore her suffering with dignity. After the war, she finally found peace as the wife of Helenus, King of Epirus.

AENEAS

In Greek mythology, **Aphrodite**'s son Aeneas was a minor Trojan warrior. But the Romans made his flight from the sack of Troy and his arrival in Rome the most important part of the story, as told in Virgil's epic poem, the *Aeneid*. To them it showed that a hero with a divine parent had been the founder of Rome.

HECUBA WITH THE BODY OF HER HUSBAND, PRIAM

PRIAM

Troy's King Priam ruled his city well, making it the most powerful in the area. But by the time of the Trojan War, Priam was an old man, who could take little part except to mourn the deaths of his sons **Achilles** and **Paris**. Priam was killed at the fall of Troy.

HECUBA

Priam's wife Hecuba bore him 50 children, but most of her sons were killed in the war. When **Paris** was born, she had a dream about Troy's destruction, so she abandoned him. But he was found and brought back to Troy. Hecuba was made a slave at the war's end.

Achilles

Hector's body

HECTOR

The Trojan leader Hector was their greatest warrior. He killed many Greeks, wounded heroes such as **Agamemnon** and **Odysseus**, and slew **Achilles**' friend **Patroclus**. When Achilles learned of Patroclus' death, the Greek hero challenged Hector to single combat. Hector hoped to tire Achilles by running three times around the walls of Troy. But Achilles caught Hector, killed him, and dragged his body three times around the walls behind his chariot in triumph.

ODYSSEY

THE *ODYSSEY*, a great epic written by the Greek poet Homer, tells of the dramatic journey made by the warrior Odysseus and his followers after the Trojan War. Because Odysseus offended the sea god Poseidon by blinding his son, the one-eyed Cyclops Polyphemus, the god prevented Odysseus from sailing home for 20 years. During the course of this long voyage, Odysseus had many adventures – with the Lotus-Eaters, the deadly sirens, the enchanting Calypso, the monster Scylla, and many more – before he reached his home at last, alone and unrecognized.

WINDS HELPING ODYSSEUS SAIL HOME TO ITHACA

Odysseus wielding a stake

THE BLINDING OF THE CYCLOPS, POLYPHEMUS

AEOLUS
The wind god, Aeolus, helped **Odysseus** on his way from the land of the **Cyclopes**. He tied up most of his winds in a goatskin and gave this to Odysseus. The only wind left blowing was the one that would take Odysseus' ships straight home to Ithaca. Odysseus' men were curious about the goatskin and, believing it contained treasure, they opened it up to look inside. The winds escaped and once more blew the Greeks off course just within sight of Ithaca. They ended up in the land of cannibal giants who ate the crew of all but one of the ships.

Sailor in animal uniform

Odysseus

Circe

THE LOTUS-EATERS
After **Odysseus** and his followers left Troy, gales blew their ships south, to the land of the Lotus-Eaters. These people ate a strange plant called the lotus, which muddled their minds and made them forget everything about their former lives. A few of Odysseus' men tried eating the plant, causing them to lose their memories and become so lethargic that they had to be carried back to their ships. But most of the crew refused the food of the Lotus-Eaters, and, with nothing to eat, Odysseus cast off and sailed away.

POLYPHEMUS
Odysseus and his men arrived in Sicily, the land of the **Cyclopes**, giant monsters with one eye in the center of their foreheads. The Greeks were looking for food and stole some sheep on the island, unaware that these animals belonged to the Cyclopes' leader, Polyphemus, who trapped the Greeks in his cave. To help his men escape, Odysseus made the Cyclops so drunk that the monster fell into a stupor. While he slept, Odysseus thrust a heated stake into the Cyclops' one eye and blinded him.

ODYSSEUS
The Greek warrior Odysseus was the King of Ithaca. Although initially reluctant to fight against the Trojans, he ended up playing a key role in the war. Famous for his cunning, it was he who designed the **Trojan Horse**, which helped the Greeks win the war. To escape from the **Cyclopes'** blinded leader, Odysseus and his followers clung to the underbellies of his sheep. As the sheep left his cave the next day, **Polyphemus** felt the backs of the sheep, but did not know the men were underneath.

ODYSSEUS THREATENING CIRCE WITH A DAGGER

CIRCE
The sorceress Circe lived on the island of Aeaea, where **Odysseus** arrived after his adventure with the **Cyclops**. Some of his crew visited Circe, who gave them a drugged drink and turned them into pigs. One man, Eurylochus, escaped and told Odysseus, who rescued the others with the help of a magic herb given to him by **Hermes**.

TIRESIAS
Circe told **Odysseus** to visit the prophet Tiresias in the under-world. Tiresias told Odysseus that he would reach Ithaca, but warned that suitors were wooing his wife.

ODYSSEUS AND HIS
CREW ESCAPING
FROM THE SIRENS

Bird's body

Odysseus tied to the mast

Woman's head

Ear filled with wax

SIRENS

On their journey, **Odysseus** and his men were attacked by the sirens. With the bodies of birds and the heads of women, these creatures were famous for their song, which was said to be so seductive that it lured sailors to shipwreck. Odysseus ordered his men to stop their ears with wax, so they would not be seduced by the sirens. But he himself wanted to hear, so he tied himself to the mast, as the ship sailed safely by.

OXEN OF THE SUN

Odysseus stopped for water in an area of the island of Sicily that was ruled by the sun god **Helios**. Some of the crew killed a few of Helios' cattle for food. This angered the god, who asked **Poseidon** to blow up a storm and shipwreck the Greeks. Odysseus was the lone survivor of the wreck, eventually landing on **Calypso**'s island.

NAUSICAA

The daughter of King Alcinous of Phaeacia, Nausicaa was on the beach with her maids when **Odysseus**, who had been shipwrecked once more, appeared and asked her for help. When Nausicaa introduced the Greek warrior to her father, Odysseus regaled him with his adventures. Alcinous lent Odysseus one of his own ships (laden with gifts), to help Odysseus return home to Ithaca.

EUMAEUS

Odysseus' most faithful servant was the swineherd Eumaeus. **Athene** told Odysseus that while his son **Telemachus** was away from Ithaca trying to find news of his father, others had taken control. The goddess told Odysseus to visit Eumaeus on his arrival in Ithaca. Eumaeus promised Odysseus that he would help him regain power.

PENELOPE

Odysseus' wife, Penelope, waited faithfully for her husband's return from the war, never believing that he was dead. Many suitors tried to persuade her to give up her wait and remarry. She told them that she would marry one of them only when she had finished work on the tapestry she was weaving, but each night she would unpick the work she had done during the day. In this way, she was able to keep all the suitors at bay until Odysseus returned.

Odysseus is caught between Scylla and Charybdis

Odysseus

Penelope

SCYLLA AND CHARYBDIS

Six-headed monster Scylla and whirlpool Charybdis lay on opposite sides of the straits between Sicily and Italy, waiting to catch innocent sailors passing by. Weighing which was more dangerous – Scylla's claws or Charybdis' swirling waters – **Odysseus** sailed his ship close to Scylla, losing six men, one to each of her ravening mouths.

CALYPSO

Enchantress Calypso, goddess of silence, lived on the floating island of Ogygia. After his ship-wreck, **Odysseus** was washed up on Ogygia's shore, where Calypso fell in love with him, wanting to marry him and make him immortal. Odysseus stayed with her for eight years, but he always longed for home and his wife **Penelope**. To please **Athene**, Calypso agreed to let Odysseus build a ship, gave him supplies, and watched him restart his journey home to Ithaca.

CALYPSO
AND ODYSSEUS

TELEMACHUS

When **Odysseus'** son saw his father so much older than he could remember, Telemachus wondered if he was an imposter. Once he was convinced of his identity, Telemachus helped his father to kill the suitors and regain the throne.

ROMAN HEROES

THE ROMAN PEOPLE HAD GREAT ADMIRATION for men of action, soldiers, and strong leaders. Many of the heroes of ancient Rome were popular because they brought glory to the city and its empire. The founders of the city of Rome were especially important, and the first seven kings were celebrated as heroic figures. The greatest Roman hero of all was Aeneas, the Trojan prince whose divine destiny it was to become king of northern Italy. Because his mother was a goddess, the Romans felt that their whole civilization had divine origins.

SIBYL AND AENEAS VISITING THE UNDERWORLD

AENEAS

Aeneas was the son of the Trojan prince Anchises and the goddess Venus. The *Aeneid*, Virgil's epic poem, tells how his adventures took him to northern Italy, where he became king, linking the Romans with their gods.

DIDO AND AENEAS
After the **Trojan War**, Aeneas and his followers sailed across the Mediterranean to North Africa. Here, Aeneas fell in love with **Dido**, queen and founder of Carthage. He wanted to stay with Dido, but the gods told him that it was his fate and duty to go to Italy. He sailed north, leaving Dido behind.

DEATH OF DIDO

Dido stabs herself

Dido was heartbroken when **Aeneas** left her. In despair, she decided to kill herself. She built a funeral pyre, and said it was a magical rite to bring Aeneas back to her. She committed suicide by climbing onto the pyre and stabbing herself.

SIBYL
There were several Sibyls, or prophetesses, in classical mythology. The most important for the Romans was the Sibyl, a priestess of **Apollo**, who lived at Cumae in Italy. The gods had made her immortal, but she became so old and shriveled that her priests hung her on the wall in a jar. When **Aeneas** visited her, she took him to the underworld, where his father **Anchises** showed him what a glorious future Rome would have.

TURNUS
Turnus, son of King Daunus and the **nymph** Venilia, was the king of the Rutili, an Italian tribe. He was engaged to Lavinia, daughter of **Latinus**. When **Aeneas** arrived in Latium, Latinus promised his daughter to the Trojan hero. Angry, Turnus waged war on Latinus and Aeneas, but was killed.

ASCANIUS
Aeneas' son Ascanius was also called Iulus. After his father's death, he became ruler of his father's city, Lavinium. He won a famous victory over the Etruscans, and then went to a place where Aeneas had sacrificed a sow and her piglets to found the city of Alba Longa, near the future city of Rome.

LATINUS
The King of Latium, Latinus, whose wife was Amata, tried to keep the peace when war broke out between **Aeneas** and **Turnus**. Amata wanted their daughter Lavinia to marry Turnus, so she encouraged Latinus to fight Aeneas. When Aeneas killed Turnus, Latium and Troy made peace.

ROMULUS AND REMUS
Romulus and Remus were the twin sons of Rhea Silvia, princess of Alba Longa. They were abandoned at birth near the Tiber River, rescued by a she-wolf, and raised by a shepherd. They wanted to build a city where they were found, but argued about the site. Romulus killed Remus and so became sole founder of Rome.

ROMULUS AND REMUS SUCKLED BY THE SHE-WOLF

LVPAE·ROMVLVM·ET·REMVM·VRBIS·CONDITORES·LACTANTIS
ANTIQVVM·AC·AENEVM·IN·CAPITOLIO·SIGNVM

ANT·LAFRERII·FORMIS·ROMAE·M·D·LII

THE RAPE OF THE SABINE WOMEN
When **Romulus** founded Rome, few people wanted to live there, particularly women. So Romulus invited the nearby Sabine tribes to come to a great feast. At a prearranged signal, Romulus' men carried off the Sabine women; then war broke out. But the women encouraged peace, and the two peoples united under Romulus.

THE LEGENDARY KINGS OF ROME

During the eighth to sixth centuries BC, Rome was ruled by a succession of seven kings, who were probably real people. Their lives and characters were described by the great first-century historian Livy, but most of his information was based on myth and folktale. So the famous seven early kings of Rome are more part of the city's mythology than its history. In Roman mythology, the role of women – either their virtue or their treachery – was of great importance in the many tales of how these great kings met their downfall.

TULLIUS HOSTILIUS, THE GREAT WARRIOR-KING

1 ROMULUS
The first Roman king ruled for 33 years, and drowned, age 54, in a storm at sea. In a vision **Romulus** said that he had become the god Quirinus.

2 NUMA
Rome's second king, Numa, founded many temples and religious cults. Numa was said to have magical powers and to have had conversations with gods such as Jupiter.

3 TULLIUS HOSTILIUS
The great warrior Tullius Hostilius was Rome's third king. He conquered the city of Alba Longa and gave Rome the strength to dominate northern Italy.

4 ANCIUS MARCIUS
The fourth king of Rome, Ancius Marcius, strengthened the city's defensive ditches and walls, increased the size of the city, and built a port at Ostia, at the mouth of the Tiber.

5 TARQUIN THE ELDER
A powerful leader, Tarquin the Elder was an Etruscan who entered Rome in an oxcart. He founded many of Rome's famous buildings, including Circus Maximus, and built a large temple to Jupiter, where everyone in Rome and the surrounding cities could worship.

6 SERVIUS TULLIUS
The sixth king of Rome carried on **Tarquin**'s work. He constructed a temple to Diana, which he copied from the one dedicated to **Artemis** in Ephesus (in modern Turkey).

7 TARQUIN THE PROUD
Tarquin was the last of the kings. He had a son called Sextus, who raped a Roman girl called Lucretia. An army of citizens chased the royal family from the city and Rome became a republic.

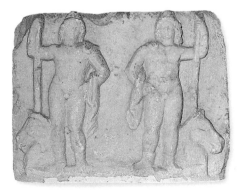

TARQUIN THE PROUD CHASED FROM ROME

EMPEROR AUGUSTUS, WHO JOKED AS HE DIED, "I THINK I'M BECOMING A GOD."

EMPERORS DEIFIED

After Julius Caesar, Dictator of Rome, died in 44 BC, Augustus came to power as the first emperor. Just as Caesar had traced his ancestry back to the legendary times of **Aeneas**, the Roman emperors who came after him claimed to be gods. It was said that an emperor became a god when he died, and sometimes his wife and children were deified too. One emperor, Caligula, claimed to be a god while he was still alive, and had statues of himself put up in the temples.

CASTOR AND POLLUX
In Greek myth, the twins Castor and Pollux were the sons of **Zeus** and **Leda**. In Roman myth, they visited a spring in the Forum at Rome, which their sister, the **nymph** Juturna, looked after. A temple to Castor was later built here.

ROMAN GODS AND GODDESSES

THE EARLY ROMANS developed their own mythology, sometimes borrowing from their neighbors, such as the Greeks (who colonized southern Italy) and the Etruscans. Many Roman gods are Greek gods with different names, but there are also differences in their characters, too. For example, Mars, the Roman god of war and equivalent to the Greek Ares, was also god of farming, while Saturn resembled the Greek Kronos but was more peaceful. The Romans borrowed some gods from other cultures, such as Cybele from Asia Minor (modern Turkey). They did have some gods of their own, such as Janus, their creator god, and their household gods, the Lares and the Penates.

SATURN

MARS, THE ROMAN GOD OF WAR

Shield carried in battle

Full battle dress

Venus

Cupid

Two-faced Janus had no Greek equivalent

SATURN
The Ancient Romans identified their god Saturn with the Greek Kronos. As Kronos had fought **Zeus**, Saturn fought Jupiter. Instead of being sent to the next world after this battle, Saturn went to Italy where he ruled in peace, teaching people farming, building, and engineering. After his death, he became the planet Saturn.

CUPID AND VENUS
The love god Cupid (Desire) was like the Greek **Eros**. But while Eros was a handsome youth, Cupid was a cherub. Known also as Amor (Love), he was often shown with his mother, the love goddess Venus. Said to be blind, he carried a bow to shoot his arrows of desire, giving little thought to his victims when he shot his arrows.

MARS
After Jupiter, Mars (the god of war, equivalent to the Greek **Ares**) was the greatest of all the Roman gods. He was conceived by **Juno**, without the aid of her husband Jupiter. Father of **Romulus and Remus**, Mars was the ancestor of all Romans, who valued his virtues – strength, bravery, and justice – most highly.

CYBELE, THE GREAT MOTHER

JANUS
Two-faced Janus, god of doorways, gates, and beginnings, gave his name to the month of January, and was the first god to be mentioned in religious ceremonies. He was sacred to soldiers, because an army had to pass through the city gates when it went into battle. Janus was also said to be the inventor of money, and early Roman coins bore his image.

CYBELE
The Greeks thought Cybele (from Phrygia in modern Turkey) was like their goddess Rhea, but the Romans worshiped her as the Great Mother, or Mother of the Gods. She was said to be accompanied by lions, who drew her chariot. The Corybantes, her attendants, danced in her honor, clashing their swords and shields. Her priests were also called Corybantes.

NATURE DEITIES

Many of Rome's most ancient gods and goddesses were nature deities, presiding over the growth and blossoming of wild flowers and the fertility and fruiting of the crops in the fields. These rural gods included Consus, god of the sowers, Tellus Mater, goddess of the fruitfulness of the soil, and Neptunus, a water god who protected the land from drought.

POMONA

The wood **nymph** Pomona lived in the forest between Rome and its port at Ostia. It was her special duty to look after the fruit trees in a wood called the Pomonal. She was beautiful, and many gods of nature and the countryside came to woo her. But Pomona loved none of them, until **Vertumnus** revealed himself to her in his true form.

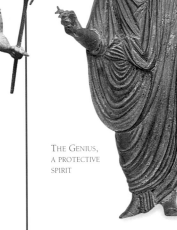

VERTUMNUS

VERTUMNUS

As the god of change, Vertumnus transformed the leaves' colors each autumn. He loved **Pomona** and visited her in different forms – as a worker, a harvester, and an old woman – to try to seduce her. Each time she rejected him, until he shook off his disguise, and she instantly fell in love with him.

FLORA, GODDESS OF FLOWERING PLANTS AND FERTILITY

FLORA

The goddess Flora presided over the spring, and made plants and trees bloom; the farmers revered her. Flora helped the goddess **Juno** conceive without her husband Jupiter. Flora had a flower that made women pregnant when they touched it. She lent this to Juno, who gave birth to **Mars**.

FAUNUS

Fertility god Faunus was an early Italian king. Like the Greek god **Pan**, he looked after shepherds. Also called Lupercus, he was honored at the festival of Lupercalia.

THE GENIUS, A PROTECTIVE SPIRIT

THE GENIUS AND THE JUNO

The Genius and the Juno were creative spirits who watched over a person from the moment of birth and presided over all the important events in a person's life. If you were a man, your creative spirit was a Genius, if a woman, it was a Juno. The spirit formed the person's character, influenced physical development, and controlled luck.

Wheel of Fortune • Blindfolded Fortuna

FORTUNA

Goddess of chance, Fortuna had a powerful influence over people's lives. This influence was unpredictable, since she was blindfolded. She had several famous symbols – a rudder to steer people's lives, a wheel to topple you to the bottom, and a cornucopia (horn of plenty) filled with fruit.

Drinking horn, a symbol of plenty

Short tunic, typical attire on Lar's statue

Food bowl

LAR, AN IMPORTANT HOUSEHOLD GOD

LARES

The Lares were a group of gods who watched over homes and crossroads. They were said to be Mercury's sons, who had a similar role. Most households had a statue to their Lar (and also to the **Penates**) in its own small shrine. The occupants made offerings to this god on important occasions, such as weddings, births, and funerals.

PENATES

The Penates were the gods of the larder. Each household had a pair to guard its food and drink. At meals it was the custom to offer the Penates food. The Penates were also a state cult and were worshiped at a Roman temple called the Velia.

VESTA

Goddess of the hearth, Vesta was like the Greek goddess **Hestia**. In Rome she was worshiped in a temple run by a group of women – the Vestal Virgins. The Vestal Virgins served in the temple for 30 years. If they broke their vow of chastity they were sentenced to death.

NORTHERN AND EASTERN EUROPE

The Norse, Finns, Celts, and Slavs had separate, and varied, mythologies. Celtic myths spread through Britain, Ireland, and France, while the extensive travels of the Norse and Germanic peoples meant that Scandinavia and Germany had similar tales of conflicts between gods and monsters. Slavic and Finnish myths include tales of nature gods and spirits.

COMMON THEMES

ODIN, RULER OF THE GODS

In spite of the variety, some common themes run through the northern myths. Each tradition has its own creation myth, with creator figures ranging from the Norse Odin to the Finnish "air-girl." Many of the stories are concerned with heroes – warriors and kings who led their people in battle and established their territory. Nature is ever present, and spirits of the forests and the rough northern seas play major roles in the stories, particularly in Scandinavia.

RECORDING THE MYTHS

People who first told the northern myths learned the stories by heart, passing them on orally. In the early Middle Ages, scholars such as Iceland's Snorri Sturlson wrote down many Norse myths. Celtic myths were also written down then. But Slavic and Finnish mythology remained unrecorded, until stories were "collected" by scholars of myth and folklore in the 19th and 20th centuries.

NORSE CREATION

IN THE BEGINNING, according to Norse mythology, there were two lands – the icy region of Niflheim in the north and the fiery realm of Muspell in the south. When the two met, they gave rise to the first giants. The universe itself was created by Odin, the ruler of the gods, and his brothers Vili and Ve. The Norse myths describe a complex creation, in which separate lands were built for the gods and mortals, as well as for giants, elves, and dwarfs. These different realms were centered around a great tree called Yggdrasil (the Tree of Life). Iceland, a country of fire and ice, is the source of the Norse myths, as chronicled in the Icelandic sagas and poems.

BERGELMIR
When **Odin**, **Vili**, and **Ve** killed **Ymir**, rivers of blood flowed from the dead **giant**'s veins. All the frost giants were drowned in the deluge except for Bergelmir and his wife, who escaped in a boat. The pair later became the parents of a new generation of giants who fought the gods.

NIGHT AND DAY
When they had created the earth from the remains of **Ymir**, gods **Odin**, **Vili**, and **Ve** gathered sparks from **Muspell** and hurled them into the sky to make the sun, moon, and stars. The three gods set these heavenly bodies on their course, determining the length of night and day.

YMIR
When warm air from **Muspell** met the cold air of **Niflheim**, the ice of Niflheim started to thaw and began to take the shape of the first **giant** – the evil Ymir. As he lay sleeping, the heat from Muspell made him sweat, and from the sweat under his left arm, two giants – one male, the other female – were formed. Another male giant appeared from his legs. This was the first generation of the frost giants, a race who made continuous war with the gods.

Melting ice thaws to form the evil giant Ymir

Male and female frost giants forming from the sweat of Ymir's left arm

Four rivers of Audhumla's milk provide food for Ymir

Odin

Vili

Ve

AUDHUMLA
The cow Audhumla was the second being in creation. She was created, like **Ymir**, from the melting ice between **Muspell** and **Niflheim**. From her udders ran four streams of milk, and these provided nourishment for the **giant**. The only food Audhumla could find for herself was the salt in the ice, which she licked greedily.

BURI AND BOR
As **Audhumla** licked the ice, a man's head was revealed. She carried on licking, until after three days, the whole man – the strong and handsome Buri – was freed from the ice. Buri's son, called Bor, married Besla, who was the daughter of one of the frost **giants**. The children of Bor and Besla were the gods **Odin**, **Vili**, and **Ve**.

ODIN, VILI, AND VE
The three creator gods – Odin, Vili, and Ve – fought the cruel **giant** Ymir and killed him. From his flesh, they created the earth; they used his teeth and bones to make rocks; with his blood they made rivers and the ocean surrounding the earth. They lifted up Ymir's skull to make the vault of the sky, and made clouds from the **giant**'s brains.

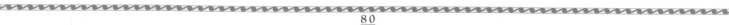

ASK AND EMBLA

The first man, Ask, and the first woman, Embla, were made by the three creators from a pair of logs on the shore of the giant sea. **Odin** gave the couple life, **Vili** gave them thoughts and feelings, and **Ve** gave them the ability to see and hear. Ask and Embla became the parents of the human race, and **Midgard** became their home.

Ask, made from an ash log

Embla

MUSPELL

A land of fire, Muspell was one of two worlds that existed before the cosmos was made. After the creation, it and its ruler, the fire **giant Surt**, were ignored by gods and men, but would fight the gods at the last battle, **Ragnarök**.

Male giant emerging from Ymir's legs

BIFRÖST

Asgard was surrounded by its great wall, but the gods needed a way in and out of their kingdom, so they built a rainbow bridge called Bifröst. The bridge was made of three strands of fire braided together, and it connected Asgard with **Midgard**. Only the gods were allowed to cross the bridge, which was guarded by the god **Heimdall** with his sword Höfud. If enemies approached Bifröst, Heimdall warned the gods with his horn Gjallar. The only mortals he would allow across Bifröst were the souls of deceased heroes who were on their way to Valhalla.

ASGARD

The gods needed a land where they could make their home, so they constructed the kingdom of Asgard – the home of the Aesir (the sky gods) and the Vanir (the earth gods, who also had a second home at Vanaheim beneath the earth). The gods wanted Asgard to be fortified, to keep out their enemies, the **giants**, as well as mortals, so they contracted a skilled craftsman to build a strong wall around Asgard in one winter. For payment, the builder demanded the sun and moon, and the goddess **Freyja** for his wife, so it seemed that he would finish the work on time. But the gods discovered that he was a giant from Jotunheim and called on **Thor**, who slew the giant with his hammer.

Ymir's eyebrows protect Midgard

Bifröst

YGGDRASIL

The different realms of Norse mythology were connected by a giant ash tree called Yggdrasil – the Tree of Life. Among the tree's three roots were the icy region of Niflheim (the realm of the dead), Jotunheim (the home of the Giants), and the home of the Norns (the rulers of human destiny). Above was Midgard, the dwelling place of humans, and higher still was Asgard, home of the gods, connected to Midgard by the bridge Bifröst.

Nidhogg, a serpent

NIDHOGG

The serpent Nidhogg lived in **Niflheim** at the foot of **Yggdrasil**. He fed on the flesh of corpses, but he also chewed on the tree's roots, trying to destroy it. The **Norns** (three old women named Fate, Being, and Necessity) healed the wounds of Yggdrasil, so Nidhogg never achieved his aim.

Raven fed off dead bodies on battlefields

YGGDRASIL

The name *Yggdrasil* may mean "horse of **Odin**," because Ygg was one of Odin's names. Odin hung on the Tree of Life for nine days – to gain knowledge of runes for writing and divination.

Eagle

YGGDRASIL – THE TREE OF LIFE

Ratatösk, Nidhogg's messenger

RATATÖSK

The squirrel Ratatösk lived in the branches of **Yggdrasil**. Ratatösk spent the whole time running up and down the tree, carrying insulting messages between the serpent **Nidhogg**, who lived at the foot of Yggdrasil, and the eagle who dwelled at the top of the Tree of Life.

HUGINN AND MUNNIN

The two ravens – Huginn (Thought) and Munnin (Memory) – were the messengers and constant companions of **Odin**. Each day the birds flew across **Midgard**, and took news about the human race back to their master.

MIDGARD

The gods made Midgard from **Ymir**'s eyebrows as a home for the humans they had created. Around Midgard, at the center of the cosmos, lay Jotunheim (the **giants'** home), Svartalfheim (home of the dark **elves**), and Nidavellir (the **dwarfs'** home).

NIFLHEIM

The frozen land of Niflheim was one of two worlds that existed before the beginning of time. It was an ice-bound land encircled by mist and shrouded in darkness, and an icy spring, Hvergelmir, was at its center. The goddess **Hel** ruled this realm of the dead.

GODS OF ASGARD

THE HOME OF THE GODS, OR ASGARD, was the highest of the three realms of the cosmos. Asgard was like a fortified citadel where the gods lived a life similar to that of people in Midgard, the home of the mortals. The gods of Asgard created the cosmos and set in motion the sun and moon. In Asgard itself, they built palaces in which to live, farmed the fields around them, and founded a court of justice. Two families of gods – the Aesir (gods of the sky) and Vanir (gods of the earth) – dwelled in Asgard. There was a great war between them, but eventually they made peace at a ceremony in which all the gods spat into a cauldron to produce a giant called Kvasir the wise. Two dwarfs killed Kvasir; from his remains they made a magic drink called the Mead of Inspiration for the gods.

Tyr's hand was bitten off by Fenrir

Odin

Sleipnir, Odin's eight-legged stallion

ODIN

The ruler of **Asgard**, Odin was god of war, storms, magic, inspiration, and the underworld. The oldest and greatest of all the Norse gods, he created the cosmos with his brothers **Vili** and **Ve**. There were two secrets to Odin's power. The first was his ability to change shape, taking any form he wished. The second was his wisdom, which he got by drinking from Mimir's well. This contained dew from one of the roots of the world's great ash tree, **Yggdrasil**.

TYR

The sky god Tyr was the son of **Odin** and **Frigg**. Bold and courageous, his role was that of general in battles that involved the gods of **Asgard**. Tyr looked after **Fenrir** the wolf, the vicious child of **Loki**, but eventually the creature bit off Tyr's hand. Tyr's other adventures included helping **Thor** capture the magic cauldron of the **giants**.

Balder

The other gods threw sticks and stones at Balder

Mistletoe spear

Loki

HOENIR

Odin's companion, the silent god Hoenir, was tall and athletic. When the sky gods in **Asgard** fought the Vanir, the earth gods took Hoenir and Mimir hostage, cut off Mimir's head, and sent it to Odin.

FRIGG

The queen of **Asgard** and the goddess of rain and fertility, Frigg wore a cloak that looked like a cloud, and she could lighten or darken in color, depending on her mood. Frigg could foretell the future, but had no power to alter it. When her beloved son **Balder** dreamed that he would come to harm, Frigg asked everything in creation not to hurt him. But she did not ask the mistletoe, and Balder was killed with a spear made from this plant.

SLEIPNIR

Odin's magical eight-legged stallion, Sleipnir, was a gift from the shape-changer **Loki**. The stallion could gallop faster than any other horse and was another source of Odin's great power. On Sleipnir, the god rode into battle, often accompanied by wolves and ravens, and galloped across the sky surrounded by the spirits of the dead.

GEFION

A giantess and one of **Frigg**'s attendants, the goddess Gefion had four sons and wanted land for them to farm. King Gylfi of Sweden promised her all the land she could plow in a day, so she turned her sons into giant oxen. They plowed a vast area before she pulled it away to make the island of Zealand.

HODER

Blind from birth, Hoder unwittingly caused his brother **Balder**'s death. **Loki** was jealous when he heard that everything in creation had vowed not to harm Balder. Loki found out that the mistletoe had not been included in the vow, and persuaded Hoder to throw a mistletoe spear at the god.

Hoder

BALDER

The son of **Odin** and **Frigg**, Balder was the most handsome of all the gods. When he was killed by the spear of mistletoe, all the gods of **Asgard** were in mourning. They persuaded **Hel** to let Balder come back to life, provided that everyone in the world wept for the dead god. Everything and everyone mourned, except for one giantess, who turned out to be **Loki** in disguise – so Balder was forced to remain in the underworld.

FORSETI

Balder's son Forseti was the god of justice, and lived in a golden palace. Whenever there was a dispute between two of the gods, they went there for Forseti to pronounce his judgment. At times he talked at such length that the gods accepted his decisions out of sheer boredom.

Hammer
Mjölnir
creates
sound of
thunder

THOR, GOD
OF THUNDER

Cone-shaped
hat

One hand
holding beard
– a symbol of
growth

FREYR, GOD OF
FERTILITY AND PLENTY

Gold
necklace
made by
the dwarfs

Clasped
breast
represents
fertility

FREYJA, GODDESS
OF FERTILITY
AND MAGIC

THOR

Big, strong, and energetic, the thunder god Thor was one of **Asgard**'s most powerful and popular deities. The thunderous sound of his hammer blows echoed across the heavens. The hammer itself, made by the **dwarfs**, could crush even the strongest opponent. Defending the gods against their enemies, the **giants**, Thor defeated giants called Thrym, who stole Thor's hammer, and Hrungir, who threatened to destroy Asgard.

SIF

Thor's wife was Sif, who was famous for her beautiful, long golden hair. One day, the trickster **Loki** cut off Sif's hair. When Thor saw Sif, he immediately flew into a violent rage. Loki was so terrified that he went to see the **dwarfs**, who made Sif some fine new hair of pure gold.

ULL

Sif's son Ull, a god with skis and a bow, was a hunter. When **Odin** was banished from **Asgard** for seducing a young woman, Ull reigned for ten years. On Odin's return to Asgard, Ull fled to Sweden, where he was worshiped.

NJÖRD AND SKÄDI

As the god of the sea, Njörd was the protector of sailors and ships. He was also the husband of Skädi, the goddess of the mountains. When they were first married Njörd and Skädi went to live together in the mountains, but Njörd could not bear to be so far away from the sea. So they moved near the ocean, but Skädi pined for the hills. Their marriage broke up. One myth says that storms are the result of Njörd's sadness at his loss of Skädi. Their children were **Freyr** and **Freyja**.

FREYR

The son of the god of the sea **Njörd** and the goddess of the mountains **Skädi**, Freyr was himself a god of plenty and fertility, and carried a sword that made him unbeatable. Freyr also had a magic ship, Skidbladnir, which could hold all the gods, but could easily be folded up when it was not in use. Freyr's sacred animal was the boar. His chariot was pulled by two of these beasts, and he also had a boar that crossed the sky every day like the sun.

Idun

Loki

Apples of Youth

FREYJA

Freyr's sister Freyja was another fertility goddess. She helped the crops grow, provided good catches for the fishermen, and came to the aid of women in childbirth. A goddess of magic and riches, she had a famous necklace called Brisingamen (made by four **dwarf** brothers called the Brisings) and a cloak of feathers called Valhamr. Freyja also stood for sexual freedom and had many lovers – both gods and mortals.

IDUN

The spring goddess Idun had a basket of apples (the Apples of Youth), which gave immortality to those who ate them. These apples were kept for the gods, but the **giants** tried to steal them. The giant Thiassi captured **Loki** and said he would release him if Loki helped him get the apples. Loki lured Idun into the forest and Thiassi captured her. When the gods began to grow old, they discovered what Loki had done. They made Loki rescue Idun and her apples, which he did by borrowing **Freyja**'s feather cloak to fly to Thiassi's home.

BRAGI

The goddess **Idun**'s husband was Bragi, who was a writer, poet, and the god of eloquence. He received his gift when **Odin** cut the runes (letters of the ancient Norse alphabet) on his tongue. Thereafter, Bragi acted as the gods' public speaker and messenger.

SEE ALSO

ASGARD 81 • DWARFS 85
FENRIR 84 • GIANTS 85
HEL 84 • LOKI 84
VE 80 • VILI 80
YGGDRASIL 81

CREATION MYTHS 8
GODS AND GODDESSES 10
HEROES AND TRICKSTERS 12
MYTHICAL MONSTERS 14
ANIMALS AND PLANTS 16
ENDINGS 18

NORSE ENEMIES

IN ADDITION TO THE GODS OF ASGARD, there were a variety of other supernatural beings in Norse mythology. Many of these were enemies of the Aesir. They plotted against the Aesir and looked forward to the chaos of the great battle of Ragnarök, which heralded the end of the world. A number of these destructive forces were unleashed by the trickster god Loki, whose practical jokes became more and more sinister. When Loki brought about the death of Odin's favorite son Balder, the trickster made matters worse by refusing to mourn, thereby condemning Balder to the underworld. After this episode, the gods chained Loki up, and he plotted the final battle, which the Norse myths say will bring the world to ruin and rebirth.

Gjall, Heimdall's hunting horn

HEIMDALL
The White God Heimdall was the watchman of **Bifröst**, the bridge that led to **Asgard**. He had sharp vision, acute hearing, and could go without sleep for days on end. But he could not speak, so **Odin** gave him a hunting horn called Gjall (Shrieker) to warn the gods of impending danger. The horn was so loud it could be heard everywhere, and Heimdall was to use it to announce the beginning of the great battle of **Ragnarök**.

SLEIPNIR
The shape-changer **Loki** disguised himself as a mare and mated with the stallion Svadilfari. As a result, Loki gave birth to Sleipnir, an eight-legged horse that could gallop at miraculous speed. Loki presented **Odin** with Sleipnir, who helped Odin enter **Niflheim**, the world of the dead, by leaping its massive gate. Odin lent the steed to his son, Hermod the Bold, who was going to Niflheim to try to rescue his brother **Balder**.

Hermod the Bold

Balder

Balldur hin Godi

Sleipnir, Odin's eight-legged horse

LOKI

Part god and part giant, Loki was a mixture of trickster and creator. He could be a friend to the gods, but Loki also caused the death of Balder. He led his monstrous children and the souls of the dead against the gods in Ragnarök, and therefore they were wary of him. His other names included the Sly God and the Father of Lies.

Loki, dragged by an eagle

BIRTH OF LOKI
The name Loki means "fire." According to one myth, Loki was created when his father Farbauti struck a flint and made a spark, which flew into the undergrowth of the island Laufey, and fire – Loki – was born. Like fire, Loki was unpredictable and changeable. A miraculous shape-changer, he could appear as a bird, a fish, a fly, a **giant**, even as a puff of smoke.

WORLD SERPENT
When the World Serpent Jormungard, the child of **Loki** and the giantess Angrboda, was born, the gods were disgusted by its appearance and threw it out of **Asgard**. The serpent lived at the bottom of the ocean, and grew so long that it curled itself all the way around **Midgard**, the world of humankind, and supported its weight.

HEL, QUEEN OF THE DEAD

HEL
The queen of the dead, Hel was sister to the **World Serpent**. The upper half of her body was alive and flesh-colored, the lower half was dead and black, hidden in the shadows of **Niflheim** and giving off the smell of rotting flesh. Hel ruled over a world of monsters, while waiting for the destruction of the gods in **Ragnarök**.

FENRIR

FENRIR
The wolf Fenrir was **Loki**'s son. The gods tried to tie him up, but he broke every one of their chains. **Odin** asked the dwarfs to make a magical band that was strong enough to hold him. Fenrir would let them put the band around his neck only if one of them showed his trust by putting his hand in his jaw. **Tyr**, a god of battle, offered his hand. The monster was tethered – but Tyr lost his right hand.

Skrymir thinks Thor's hammer blows are falling acorns

Thor hits the giant Skrymir on the head with his hammer

GIANTS

The giants, or trolls, were the first creatures to appear in the universe. They lived everywhere, in storm clouds, in mountains, even in the sea. Although they could be friendly, giants were feared for their size, their warlike characters, and their destructive powers – erupting like volcanoes, causing storms at sea, and making the earth shake. They even defied the gods.

SURT

Before the creation of the cosmos, there existed **Muspell**, a world of fire ruled by a **giant** called Surt. People believed that at **Ragnarök**, Surt would erupt like a volcano, throwing fire to the four corners of the world, to destroy everything.

ELVES

There were two types of elves: light elves and dark elves. The dark elves made the fetter with which the gods bound **Fenrir**. It was made from the sound of a cat's footfall, a woman's beard, a mountain's roots, a bear's sinews, a fish's breath, and a bird's spittle.

DWARFS

Created from the maggots in the flesh of the frost **giant Ymir**, **dwarfs** were wise, but could be tricked. Their leader was called Modsognir. They lived underground, and were skilled craftspeople and metalworkers. They made **Thor**'s hammer and other treasures of the gods.

THE RIDE OF THE VALKYRIES

VALKYRIES

The Valkyries were immortal women and the servants of **Odin**. They brought the souls of the heroes who were killed in battle to Valhalla (The Hall of the Slain), Odin's great hall in **Asgard**. There the heroes practiced feats of arms, in preparation for **Ragnarök**, when they would fight on the side of the gods.

NORNS

The Norns controlled human fate, by weaving into their tapestries the destinies of the people on earth. There were three Norns: Skuld, Urd, and Verdandi. Skuld was resentful if people insulted the Norns, and would tear up the tapestry. Skuld's action brought chaos and confusion to life on earth.

RAGNARÖK

The last battle between the gods and their enemies was called Ragnarök, The Twilight of the Gods. In this battle, **Loki** would escape, destroy **Bifröst**, and lead the **giants** against the gods of **Asgard**. The wolf **Fenrir** would gobble up **Odin**, and **Thor** would kill the **World Serpent**, perishing from its poison in the process. The old world of the gods would be destroyed in the end, and a beautiful new world would begin.

VALI

The god Vali was a son of **Odin**. He became a hero when he was only one day old and he resolved to avenge the death of his brother **Balder**, the favorite son of Odin and his wife **Frigg**. Vali slayed **Höder** with his bare hands, and placed the body on a funeral pyre. Vali was one of the deities who would survive the battle of **Ragnarök**, and with another brother, **Vidar**, would become a god of the new world that was to follow.

VIDAR

Odin's son, the silent and slow-witted Vidar, would kill the wolf **Fenrir** at the battle of **Ragnarök**. A survivor, he was to become a god in the new world.

FINNISH MYTHS

IN THE EARLY 19TH CENTURY, the Finnish scholar Elias Lönnrot traveled his country collecting folk songs about Finland's ancient gods and heroes. He wrote these down, making a long, continuous epic that he called the *Kalevala*. The *Kalevala* deals with the story of the creation and the deeds of various heroes, chief among whom are the prophet Väinämöinen and the quester and trickster Lemminkäinen. Part of the epic tells of the struggle for the Sampo – a mystical device described as a combination of corn mill, salt mill, and money mill. But the Sampo was more magical than a mere machine. It was the key to prosperity and good fortune to any who possessed it. The epic ends by looking forward to the coming of the mortal kings, and the founding of the independent Finnish state.

Wild duck nesting

LUONNOTAR

The air-girl Luonnotar was the goddess who created the world over thousands of years. One day a wild duck landed on her knee, made its nest, and laid seven eggs. As they hatched, the heat was unbearable for the air-girl, so she moved to shake them off. The eggs fell into the water and turned into the earth (islands and mainland), heavens, sun, moon, stars, and clouds.

Väinämöinen — *Louhi*

NATURE SPIRITS

Many Finnish gods represented the world of nature, especially the dense forests and cold seas of Finland. For example, Tapio, the forest god, had a whole family of woodland deities, whom the local people worshiped to ensure that they would be successful when hunting in the woods.

LAKES AND FORESTS IN FINLAND

DEVILS AND DEMONS
Finnish mythology is full of evil spirits who fight heroes such as **Väinämöinen**. A trio of evil spirits made Väinämöinen injure himself with his own axe: Hiisi made the axe shake in the hero's hand; Lempo turned the blade toward his flesh; and Paha pushed it toward his knee.

LOUHI
The princess of the Northland was Louhi, a witch and terrifying frost giantess. She asked **Väinämöinen** to make the **Sampo**, which Louhi hoped would bring prosperity to her frozen land. But when she tried to snatch the Sampo from Väinämöinen, it broke into pieces, and her northern realm stayed cold and barren.

PELLERVOINEN
The god Pellervoinen was born out of the earth. **Väinämöinen** called upon him to plant trees and flowers over the earth, and Pellervoinen became the deity of trees, plants, and the fields. When the trees grew, Väinämöinen cut most of them down to plant barley. But he left a single birch tree so that the birds had somewhere to roost.

AHTO
The water god Ahto lived with his water goddess wife Vellamo and their daughters in a hollow black cliff lashed by the waves. His swirling whirlpools and water spirits posed dangers to sailors if they did not pray to the gods of the waters.

TAPIO
The god of the forests was called Tapio. His cloak was made of moss, and his beard and hat of trees. He gave his name to Finland, which used to be called Tapiola.

VÄINÄMÖINEN
The god of song and poetry, Väinämöinen was the great prophet of Finnish mythology. Born of **Luonnotar** who bore him for more than 700 years, he is often portrayed as an old man who plays the kantele, a stringed instrument. His main adventures include visiting **Tuonela** to find magic spells and struggling with **Louhi**.

AINO
When **Väinämöinen** was challenged by Joukahäinen, the two threw incantations and spells at each other. Väinämöinen cornered the Laplander in a swamp. To get free, Väinämöinen promised the god the hand of his sister Aino. But Aino did not love the god, who was much too old for her. Rather than marry Joukahäinen, she dived into the sea and turned into a mermaid.

Aino — *Väinämöinen*

Ilmarinen forging the Sampo from a swan's feather

ILMARINEN AND THE SAMPO

The blacksmith god Ilmarinen was the only person who could make the Sampo, and **Louhi** promised him the hand of her daughter in return for it. But when the smith produced the Sampo, Louhi locked it away. **Väinämöinen**, Ilmarinen, and **Lemminkäinen** managed to retrieve the Sampo, but as Louhi tried to grab it from them, both she and the Sampo fell into the water. Only one part of the Sampo remained, grinding out salt at the bottom of the ocean.

TUONELA

Tuonela, the Finnish underworld, was ruled by Tuoni, god of the dead. It was circled by a river, on which swam the black swan that **Lemminkäinen** wanted to kill. Tuonela was like the world of the living, but was dark and silent, and full of demons and diseases brought about by Tuoni.

MARJATTA

At the end of the *Kalevala*, the maiden Marjatta had a son, who became Finland's king. **Väinämöinen** made way for him, leaving the country – and his kantele – behind for ever.

LEMMINKÄINEN

The hero Lemminkäinen, son of the love goddess Kylliki, wandered the world in search of a wife. **Louhi** promised him her daughter's hand if he could perform three tasks: overtake the elk of the demon Hiisi, the fastest beast in the cosmos; put a bridle on a fire-breathing horse; and shoot the swan of **Tuonela**. Lemminkäinen managed the first two, but he was choked by a water snake in Tuonela before being killed by Tuoni, god of the dead. His mother then restored him to life.

Kullervo on the warpath against evil Louhi

KULLERVO

Separated from his family, Kullervo became one of **Louhi**'s slaves. Louhi ill-treated Kullervo, but he got his own back by turning her cattle into bears and wolves. The animals tore Louhi limb from limb, but Kullervo managed to escape. He met and fell in love with a slave-girl, but then discovered that she was his long-lost sister. In despair, the pair committed suicide together.

SIBERIA

The Siberians have their own creation story. The sky god Ulgan made the first created being, Erlik, from mud. Both Ulgan and Erlik were shape-changers and often flew through the air as a pair of geese. Ulgan asked Erlik to dive down to the bottom of the ocean to collect mud, with which Ulgan could create the earth. Erlik kept some mud in his beak, hoping to make his own world, but when Ulgan ordered the mud to expand, Erlik had to spit the mud out.

Ulgan

Newly created Erlik rising to the muddy surface

ULGAN AND ERLIK

One day, when flying, Erlik went too high, plummeted into the water, and started to sink. In danger of drowning, Erlik called for help. Ulgan pulled him out of the water, ordering a stone to come to the surface so that Erlik had something to sit on.

THE MAID OF THE NORTH

Louhi, ruler of Pohjola (or the Northland), had a daughter, the Maid of the North. When heroes came to Louhi to ask permission to marry her daughter, Louhi set them many impossible tasks.

SLAVIC MYTHS

THE SLAVIC PEOPLES live in a large area of central and eastern Europe, from Poland in the north to Serbia and Macedonia in the south. The father of the Slavic gods was Svarog (the sky god), and his children included Dazhbog (the sun god) and Svarogich (the fire god). Many of the most popular Slavic gods were local spirits of the woods, rivers, and fields. These, like the household gods, were said to work mischief on the lazy or unwary; mishaps and problems, from burned food to an accident on the road, were said to be the work of the spirits. The Slavic peoples also had heroes (bogatyrs), whose stories are mixed up with Christian ideas and were first written down in the ninth century.

DUAL SLAVIC GODS
REPRESENTING OPPOSITE FORCES

PAIRS OF GODS
Since the earliest times, pairs of opposite gods – good and evil – have been common in Slavic mythology. One of the most ancient pairings is Byelobog and Chernobog. Dressed in white, Byelobog was the force for good and creation, and he was always in conflict with Chernobog, the black-cloaked lord of evil and destruction. The pair may have come to the Slavic world from western Asia, and are similar to **Ahura Mazda** and **Angra Mainyu** of Persia.

MATI-SYRA-ZEMLYA
The Slavic earth goddess was called Mati-Syra-Zemlya (Moist Mother Earth). People worshiped her by digging a hole in the ground, then speaking into the hole. Listening to the sounds from the hole was one way of telling if the goddess was going to bring a good harvest.

BABA YAGA
The terrifying Baba Yaga, goddess of death, had a deadly glance that turned humans to stone. When she killed people, she took the bodies home, brought them back to life, and devoured them. She kept only the bones, which she used to build her house. Baba Yaga rode in a large mortar, using the pestle to propel her through the sky.

KOSHCHEI THE DEATHLESS
The brutal demon Koshchei was the male counterpart of **Baba Yaga**. Koshchei was able to escape death until he came to the fateful oak tree. Koshchei, who was sometimes depicted as a serpent or dragon, kept his life in an egg inside a duck inside a hare inside a casket, all hidden under an oak tree. When the hero prince Ivan found and smashed the egg, Koshchei was killed. The name Koshchei means "old bony."

PERUN
The god of thunder and lightning, Perun was a creative deity who brought fertility and life-giving rain to the fields. He was associated with oak trees, and was portrayed as a wooden statue with a silver head and a gold moustache. In his other role as a war god, he rode across the sky in a chariot drawn by a giant goat, wielding his lightning bolt. The dragon symbolized Perun, and paganism.

BOGATYRS

The heroes, or bogatyrs, described in old Russian epic poems are some of the most colorful characters of Slavic mythology. Their stories concern the bogatyrs' magical strength and the way in which they bravely protect their homeland. Later, the bogatyrs became heroes of the Christian religion.

SVYATOGOR
The hero Svyatogor thought he could lift the earth. One day he found a tiny bag so heavy he could only lift it to his knees. As he did so, he sank into the earth. He struggled to get out till he wept tears of blood, but was stuck and starved to death.

ILYA-MUROMYETS
A sickly child, Ilya-Muromyets gained his strength as a young man from a magic drink that some minstrels gave him. His heroic deeds included fighting a bird-headed demon who caused hurricanes. In later times, he became a Christian hero and defended the faith.

RUSALKAS
The souls of infants or drowned girls were known as rusalkas. Taking the form of attractive young maidens, they lived in watery places and were said to have a beautiful song, which they used to entice men to a watery death.

NATURE GODS

In ancient eastern and central Europe, few people traveled far from their native villages, so forests and lakes were unfamiliar and threatening places, especially at night. Nature spirits who misdirected or attacked travelers, or tricked them into the water, helped to explain why people were terrified.

Dvorovoi

RUSTIC GODS

Country people believed in a host of spirits living in and around the farm. They included Dvorovoi, god of the yard, who hated animals with white coats, especially cats and horses; Bannik, spirit of the wash house, who could foretell the future; and Ovinnik, spirit of the barns, who looked like a black cat.

VAMPIRE ATTACKING HELPLESS VICTIM

VAMPIRES

Undead corpses who refused to give up life were known as vampires. They needed to drink human blood in order to stave off death, and wandered about the countryside at night looking for sleeping victims. To kill a vampire, a victim had to stab it through the heart with a crucifix or expose the creature to daylight. The famous vampire, Dracula, was a fictional character based on Vlad the Impaler, the Prince of Walachia.

POLEVIKS

Field spirits called poleviks hid in the corn and jumped out to misdirect travelers or kill drunken farm workers. Their bodies were the color of earth, their hair like green grass. Female poleviks took the form of beautiful women dressed in white. They would take farm workers' children and lose them among the corn. An offering of two eggs and an old cockerel, placed at the edge of the field, kept a polevik at bay.

HOUSEHOLD GODDESSES

KIKIMORA

The Slavs had several household goddesses who helped with work around the home. One of these spirits, Kikimora, was said to give assistance if the woman of the house was a hard worker. But if she was lazy, Kikimora would make mischief in the kitchen and would also keep the woman's children awake at night by tickling them. To put things right, the housewife had to make a special tea from ferns, then use it to scrub out all the kitchen pots. Another household goddess was Dugnai, who helped to bake bread.

LESHY

The forest spirit Leshy could vary in size from a dwarf to a giant, but was always known by his long green beard. He liked to mislead anyone who ventured into the forest, but canny travelers knew that they could be free of him by removing their clothes and putting them on backward.

VODYANOI

A slimy, male water spirit – the vodyanoi – lived in a palace made from crystal and parts of boats that had sunk to the bottom of a lake. The vodyanoi came to the surface at night to drag unwary travelers deep into the lake, where they drowned and became the spirit's slaves.

KURENT AND KRANYATZ

A Serbian myth describes how the giant Kranyatz survived the great flood. He was helped by the trickster god Kurent, who let Kranyatz hang onto his stick made from a vine. When Kranyatz thanked Kurent, Kurent said that Kranyatz should thank the vine and the two argued about who should rule the world. The giant won a trial of strength and became ruler, but Kurent vowed revenge. Kurent tried to make Kranyatz drunk, but was unsuccessful until he added his blood to the wine and Kranyatz became inebriated at God's table. God became angry, Kranyatz lost his strength, and Kurent ruled the world after all.

Kurent filling Kranyatz's drinking horn to make him drunk

WEREWOLVES

People born with a birthmark or a caul, were often thought to be werewolves – beings who could change themselves at will into wolves. Werewolves were especially active at a full moon. One origin of this myth is an 11th-century prince from Belarus called Vseslav, who was said to transform himself into a wild beast rampaging on the battlefield.

YARILO

Yarilo was the god of sexuality and fertility. He was especially worshiped in the spring, when one of the village maidens was crowned as his queen in the hope that newly planted seed would bear rich fruit.

CELTIC MYTHOLOGY

THE TERM CELTIC IS NORMALLY USED for the peoples who lived in Britain and western Europe between 500 BC and AD 400. They were Iron Age peoples who lived mainly in small villages and were led by warrior chiefs. The Celts of continental Europe left no written records, but we know about their gods from the Romans, who conquered their lands. The Romans linked many of these deities with their own. For example, the thunder god Taranis was equivalent to the Roman Jupiter, and many different local deities were identified with Mars, Mercury, and Apollo. The peoples of Wales and Ireland also left a rich fund of myths. Many of their tales were written down during the Middle Ages, so we know more about their gods and heroes than those of the European mainland.

SUCELLUS
Sometimes described as the king of the gods, the fertility deity Sucellus carried a big, long-handled hammer, and his name means The Good Striker. He used his hammer to strike the earth, waking up the plants and heralding the beginning of spring. His wife was the water goddess Nantosuelta (Winding River), another fertility figure, who was also goddess of hearth and home.

SUCELLUS AND HIS CONSORT NANTOSUELTA

TRIPLE MOTHER GODDESS

Silver wheel

TARANIS
The thunder god Taranis rode across the sky in his chariot. Lightning was produced by sparks from his horses' hooves, and thunder came from the sound of his chariot wheels. He was worshiped widely in the Celtic world, and he may have been linked with the Roman sky god Jupiter, who carried a thunderbolt.

TARANIS, THE THUNDER GOD

EPONA AND HER HORSE

EPONA
Goddess of the earth and one of the most popular Celtic deities, Epona was usually shown with a horse. The horse's vigor and strength was a symbol of the power of the earth and its fertility. White horse figures cut into chalky hills may have been dedicated to Epona.

TRIPLE MOTHER
The Celtic mother goddess is often depicted as three women, each holding different items, such as a dog, a fish, and a basket of fruit. Three was a sacred number for the Celts, and triple figures, or three-headed gods, were usual.

BELANUS
The Celts had several gods of fire and light, shown by the word Bel (Shining) in their names. They included Belatucadrus, a war god linked to the Roman **Mars**, and Belanus, a sun god identified with **Apollo**. The Celts may have seen them as aspects of the same god.

CERNUNNOS
One of the most ancient Celtic gods was Cernunnos, The Horned One. He had the ears and antlers of a stag and was seen as a lord of the beasts. Often portrayed with animals such as snakes and stags, Cernunnos was sometimes shown feeding them. This indicates that he was a god of plenty and fertility. Cernunnos was also a shape-changer, and could take the form of a snake, wolf, or stag.

Antlers

Torc

Torc, or collar

Stag, symbol of sexuality

Cernunnos

Breeches

Ram-headed snake, symbol of regeneration

WALES

The Welsh myths are gathered in a collection called the *Mabinogion*. The book has four Branches – the tales of Pwyll (king of Dyfed and his family), Branwen (the god Llyr and his family), Manawydan (in which Lyr and Pwyll's families are united), and Math (the family of Dôn, mother of the gods).

Princess Rhiannon riding her wild white horse

RHIANNON
Princess Rhiannon first appeared to Pwyll on a wild white horse. She married the king and bore his son, Pryderi. When the child disappeared, she was accused of his murder. As a punishment, she had to carry visitors into the palace. Later Pryderi reappeared, so Rhiannon was released from her penance.

BRANWEN
Daughter of the sea god Llyr, the beautiful Branwen married the king of Ireland, but was ill-treated. She sent a message to Wales telling of her fate, so the Britons declared war on Ireland.

BENDIGEIDFRAN
Bendigeidfran (Brân the Blessed) was a giant son of Llyr. He led the Britons to victory against the Irish and was killed, but his severed head remained alive, to entertain his followers

Lleu Llaw Gyffes as an eagle

Blodeuwedd

BLODEUWEDD
Warrior hero Lleu Llaw Gyffes' mother, Arianrhod, said he should never marry a human, so Math, lord of Gwynedd, and the magician Gwydion created the beautiful, but unfaithful Blodeuwedd from flowers. She and her lover Gronw Pebyr planned to kill Lleu, who escaped by changing into an eagle.

IRELAND

Irish myth tells of five invasions that occurred before the Celts arrived. The last invasion was by a divine race called the Tuatha Dé Danann. Many of the most popular stories in Irish mythology involve members of the Tuatha Dé Danann. Another group of stories concerns the great hero of Ulster – Cuchulain – who fought the men of Connacht.

The Daghda

LUGH'S MAGIC BOAT

MANANNAN MAC LIR
The sea god Manannán, one of the Tuatha Dé Danann, was the patron of Ireland and protector of Irish heroes. He gave **Lugh** a magic boat, sword, and horse, to help him fight off invaders.

MORRIGAN
The war goddess Morrigan could change from human to animal shape. When she appeared as a raven, death was nearby – and if she washed a warrior's armor, the man would die. She was also a goddess of sexuality and tried to seduce the hero **Cuchulain**.

CUCHULAIN
The warrior hero Cuchulain was said to be the son of the god **Lugh**. He fought bravely with the men of Ulster against the warriors of Connacht, laying men low with his fearsome barbed spear. He was killed by his own spear thrown by one of the sons of the warrior Cailidin, in revenge for the death of their father. He tied himself to a stone pillar so that he would die fighting.

CUCHULAIN, ULSTER'S WARRIOR HERO

LUGH
God of sunshine and light, Lugh (the Shining God) was a warrior, craftsman, and magician. He created many magic weapons, including a sword that could cut through anything. In a battle against the Formorians, Lugh killed their leader, his grandfather Balar.

THE DAGHDA
God of magic, wisdom, and fertility, the Daghda (the Good God) was one of the Tuatha Dé Danann. His vast cauldron provided food for the gods. He also had a magic club, one end of which could kill people – the other end could bring the dead back to life.

FINN
Hunter, prophet, and leader of the warriors, the Fenians, Finn achieved great wisdom when he licked his thumb, burned when he was cooking the Salmon of Knowledge. Among his heroic deeds, he hunted magic boars and saved Tara, home of the Irish kings, from a goblin.

OISIN
Finn's son Oisin lived in the Land of Youth. He was allowed to visit Ireland only if he did not step on its soil, but he fell from his horse and immediately aged 300 years.

KING ARTHUR

THE MYTHICAL KING ARTHUR, famed as Britain's brave and virtuous leader, was probably based on a real person. He may have been a British leader in the Dark Ages, just after the Romans left Britain in the fifth century. During medieval times, different writers, such as the Frenchman Chrétien de Troyes and the Briton Thomas Malory, wrote about Arthur, retelling the ancient myths about the Knights of the Round Table who met at Arthur's court at Camelot. They chronicled his chivalry, told of the events leading to his death, and looked to the time when the "once and future king" would rule again, presiding over a golden age.

KING ARTHUR

Arthur

Sir Ector

ARTHUR PULLS THE SWORD FROM THE STONE

Sir Kay

EXCALIBUR

After **Arthur**'s first sword was broken, **Merlin** took Arthur to the **Lady of the Lake**. Her hand appeared above the water, brandishing a new sword – Excalibur. The king kept this sword, which rendered him unbeatable in battle, until the end of his life, when he gave Excalibur to Sir Bedivere to throw back into the lake. The Lady's hand caught the sword, and a barge arrived to take Arthur to **Avalon**.

Excalibur, handed over by the Lady of the Lake

Arthur

LANCELOT

The bravest of the knights, Lancelot was guilty of betrayal when he slept with **Guinevere**, and was found unworthy to go on the quest for the **Holy Grail**. Later, Lancelot gave away his property to the church and became a monk.

AVALON

The island of Avalon was a happy land in the West. The name Avalon means Island of Apples, and it was here that the apples of immortality grew. **Arthur** was taken to Avalon at the end of his earthly life to heal his wounds. There he fell into eternal sleep until he will be woken up to save Britain in its hour of need.

ARTHUR

Son of Igraine, queen of Cornwall, and the Welsh prince Uther Pendragon, Arthur became king of Britain. Famous as an ideal monarch, Arthur ruled wisely and bravely, uniting Britain and governing his country peacefully with the help of the Knights of the **Round Table**. But the adultery between his wife **Guinevere** and **Lancelot**, and the treachery of Arthur's son **Mordred**, brought strife to his reign. Arthur died of his wounds when fighting Mordred. But his death was not final. One day he will return to rule Britain once again.

SWORD IN THE STONE

Arthur showed himself worthy to be king of Britain when he was still a boy. His father Uther Pendragon had embedded a sword in a great stone, and Arthur was the only person able to pull it out. He kept the sword, and fought bravely with it. Finally, it was broken in a fight with a giant.

GUINEVERE

The beauty of Guinevere, **Arthur**'s queen, attracted all the Knights of the **Round Table**, but only **Lancelot** broke his vows of chivalry, to commit adultery with her – this act led to the breakup of the Round Table. For her betrayal, Guinevere was condemned to be burned at the stake, but Lancelot rescued her, killing two knights. To avenge these deaths, their brothers, Arthur and **Gawain**, declared war on Lancelot. The Knights of the Round Table had to take sides in the bitter struggle that followed. Meanwhile, **Mordred** seized the throne of England and declared himself king.

MORGAN LE FAY

The mysterious fairy creature Morgan le Fay was usually seen as an evil figure, plotting against **Arthur** to bring about the downfall of the human race. Morgan le Fay was Igraine's daughter and Arthur's half-sister. Her sister, Morgause, was **Mordred**'s mother.

LADY OF THE LAKE

Around **Avalon** was a magical lake with an underground castle, dwelling place of the Lady of the Lake. A protector of humanity, she looked after **Arthur**. She gave him **Excalibur**, tended his last wounds, and took him to Avalon to die.

ROUND TABLE

Arthur and his knights sat at a large round table (a wedding gift from **Guinevere**'s father). Medieval courtiers generally used long, rectangular tables, but this arrangement encouraged rivalry, with knights vying for the best position nearest the king at the center. With a round table, all the knights had equal status with each other.

KING ARTHUR AND THE KNIGHTS OF THE ROUND TABLE

MORDRED RIDES OUT TO FACE ARTHUR AT THE BATTLE OF CAMLANN

MORDRED

An illegitimate son of **Arthur**, Mordred grew up away from Camelot, but returned as a knight. Mordred plotted against Arthur, when he was away fighting. He tried to trick the knights, saying that Arthur was dying of his wounds and that he should take over and marry **Guinevere**. She sent a message to Arthur. He returned, fought Mordred, and both men met their deaths.

GALAHAD

The purest of **Arthur**'s knights was Galahad, son of **Lancelot** and Elaine. He was the model of virtue and obedience, and was looked upon by Christian writers as a symbol of Christ. Galahad was born because of a trick. Pelles, ruler of the kingdom of Carbonek, made Lancelot mistake his daughter Elaine for **Guinevere**. Galahad was born as a result of this union. It was his destiny to search for the **Holy Grail**. After many adventures and struggles against evil, with his fellow knights Perceval and Bors, Galahad found the grail and returned it to Jerusalem. Here he died in ecstasy, and was taken up to heaven.

Galahad

Perceval

AT THE COURT OF KING PELLES

GAWAIN

To test **Arthur**'s men, **Morgan le Fay** changed Lord Bertilak into a Green Knight. He challenged Gawain to a beheading contest. Gawain beheaded the Knight, who picked up his head, telling Gawain to meet him a year later at a chapel. On the way Gawain met Bertilak, whose wife tried to seduce him. He resisted, went to the chapel, and met the Knight, who made as if to behead Gawain. Turning into Bertilak, he praised Gawain for his bravery and virtue.

NIMUE OR VIVIEN

The shape-changer Nimue (also known as Vivien) was said to be the daughter of a **siren** from Sicily. The foster-mother of **Merlin**, Nimue also became his lover. When she had seduced him, she turned herself into amber, to trap the hapless wizard with her for ever in an enchanted wood called Broceliande. According to Thomas Malory, Nimue went with Guinevere, who escorted **Arthur** to Avalon. She is therefore sometimes confused with the **Lady of the Lake**.

NIMUE

MERLIN

Said to be the son of a nun and a demon, the wizard Merlin was brought up by **Nimue** (also known as **Vivien**), whom he taught much of his magic. He brought together **Arthur**'s parents, and when their son was born looked after his education and made the **Round Table**. Nimue loved Merlin and used magic powers to seduce him. At first Merlin resisted, but he was trapped by Nimue when she turned herself into a beautiful woman.

THE BEGUILING OF MERLIN

Merlin

Nimue

THE HOLY GRAIL

The most precious of all Christian relics was the Holy Grail. According to the usual version of the story, the Grail was the cup used by Jesus at the Last Supper. Another account says that the Grail was the bowl into which Christ's blood dripped when he was on the cross. In each case, the Grail was said to have been given to Joseph of Arimathea, but had been lost. Many went in search of it, but the most famous of all Grail questers were King **Arthur**'s knights. Since the Grail was thought to disappear if an impure person went anywhere near it, only the purest knights, such as **Galahad**, were thought worthy to search for it.

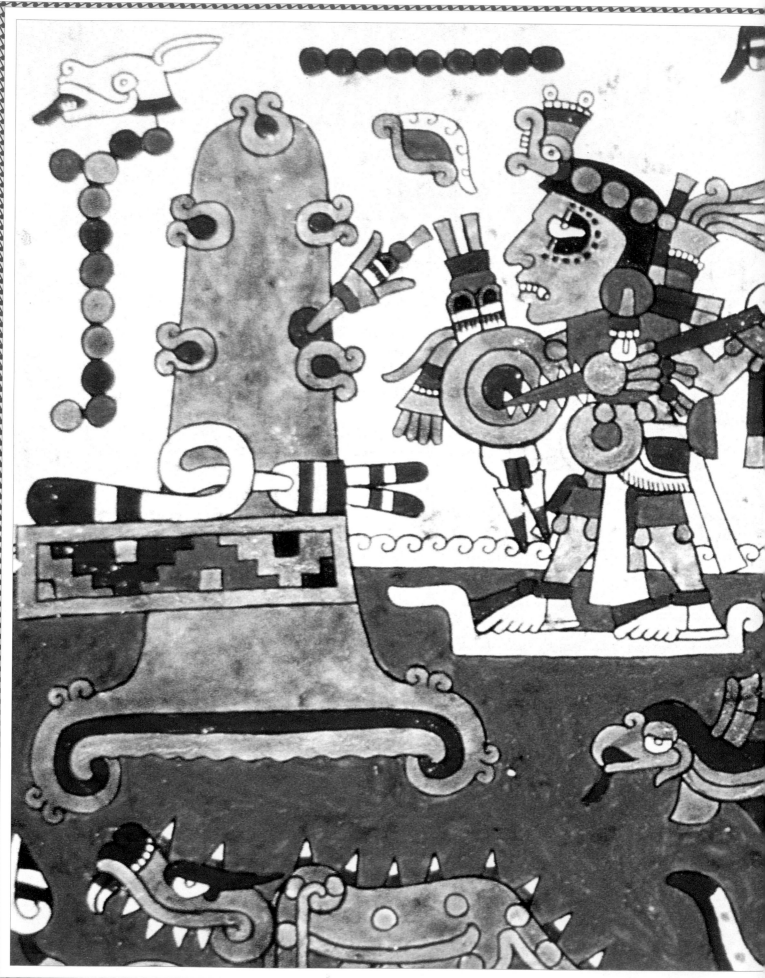

THE AMERICAS

People arrived in North America at least 12,000 years ago and gradually spread southward to present-day South America, taking their stories with them and adapting the tales to match the varied environments they found in different parts of the continent.

ARCTIC OCEAN
Inuit
NORTH AMERICA
Northwest
PACIFIC OCEAN
East
Plains
ATLANTIC OCEAN
Southwest
CENTRAL AMERICA
Aztec
Maya
Inca
SOUTH AMERICA

CULTURE AND ENVIRONMENT

The hundreds of different Native North American peoples are usually grouped into cultural areas that reflect their lifestyles, which vary according to the geography. This book uses a simplified version of the system. The people of the Arctic lived from hunting and fishing, the Plains Indians herded buffalo, and in the Southwest, artisans created distinctive designs.

CENTRAL AND SOUTH AMERICA

The civilizations of Central and South America had complex organized religions, and worshiped their gods in large stone temples. Humans were often sacrificed as part of their rituals. Weather gods – from the rain deities of the Aztecs to the sun god of the Incas – were important to these people, who often lived in places where conditions were harsh and food supplies depended on the climate.

FROM CREATORS TO TRICKSTERS

COYOTE

Native Americans created a rich variety of mythical figures – from the trickster Coyote, whose entertaining antics explain hardship and death in the world, to the Pawnee creator figure One Above, who presides over all the cosmos.

INUIT

THE PEOPLES OF THE CANADIAN ARCTIC are known as the Inuit, which means "people." The Arctic is an inhospitable world of freezing winds, ice, and snow, where it is impossible to grow crops, and hunting and fishing are the traditional sources of food. Inuit mythology is heavily influenced by this harsh environment, where people depend on animals for clothing, tools, and shelter, as well as food. Everywhere animals play a key part in the myths – as helpers of humankind and as quarry to which the hunter must show the greatest respect. The world of the sea is also important, and many Inuit peoples have a myth involving a sea woman, Sedna, who is known as Mother of Sea Beasts and guards all creatures in the sea.

NORTHERN LIGHTS

AURORA BOREALIS
When the aurora borealis appears, the Koyukon from western Alaska believe that it is Northern Lights Man shooting arrows across the winter sky. This pleases the hunters, because caribou, on which they depend, will soon arrive. The flashing lights are also said to be the dancing spirits of the dead.

PINGA (PANA)
A hunting goddess, Pinga plays an important part in the lives of northern peoples, such as the Caribou Inuit. She watches over the caribou, herding them together and directing them toward the hunters. Souls of the dead are reborn in the house of Pinga (The Woman Up There).

IKULA NAPPA
The Inuit equivalent of European mermaids, Ikula Nappa is half-woman, half-fish. Dwelling at the bottom of the sea, she is a shadowy figure, sometimes confused with the **Sea Woman**.

SEA WOMAN
Sea Woman is another name for **Sedna**. She guards her sea friends, blowing up storms if humans offend her. When this occurs, a shaman dives into the sea to clean her hair, since she has no fingers to do this for herself.

A SHAMAN FIGURINE

SHAMANS
The priests of North American religions – the shamans – were the only people who had any control over the spirit world. In their ceremonies they could influence the spirits to help heal the sick and to bring success to fishermen and hunters. The first shamans were called Ivivarshuk and Nisguvaushaq.

Sea creatures form from Sedna's fingers

SEDNA
The sea spirit Sedna (Mother of Sea Beasts) lives beneath the oceans. Here she guards and looks after all sea creatures, particularly the seals. She began life as a mortal woman, but refused to take a human husband – she married a dog instead. The people thought this would bring bad luck, so they took her out to sea in a boat, hoping to throw her overboard. But she clung on to the boat, and the men chopped off her fingers. Sedna fell into the water and became the ruler of the underworld. Her fingers became seals and other sea creatures, such as dolphins and walruses.

SEDNA SINKING TO THE BOTTOM OF THE SEA

SIBERIAN WOLF

Feather

Fur

DECORATED WESTERN ALASKA INUIT FINGER MASK

INUA
The northern peoples believe that almost everything has its own soul, or "inua." Animals, rocks, trees, and rivers have inua, as do dangerous features of the landscape, such as glaciers or whirlpools. The inua is usually portrayed as a human face on an animal's eye, back, or breast. Careful travelers must make offerings of meat to the inua.

AKHLUT
People near the Bering Sea fear the killer whale, Akhlut, who can change his shape into a wolf. In this form he lopes across the land, killing and devouring people and animals. Once he has eaten his fill, he goes back to the shore and turns himself into a killer whale again. Wolf tracks leading to the sea are thought to be a sign that Akhlut has been on the prowl.

TULUNGERSAK, OR
FATHER RAVEN

TULUNGERSAK

Father Raven, or
Tulungersak, began as
a human figure. He
stumbled about the
earth and made a
figure like himself from
the clay he found
around him. But the
creature was restless,
so Tulungersak threw
it into the void, where
it became an evil spirit.
Tulungersak wanted to
explore the sky, so he
made himself wings,
turning into a raven.
He created humans
from clay, planted
herbs and flowers,
made animals, taught
men how to hunt and
fish, and made light
and darkness.

TINMIUKPAK

For the Yukon delta
people, Tinmiukpak is
the Thunderbird – an
enormous eagle that
can produce claps of
thunder by beating its
wings. It is so large
that it can pick up
reindeer and whales
in its talons, and is also
said to kill humans.

EAGLE'S GIFT

At first humans spent
all their time working.
Then an eagle made
friends with a man
called Ermine, and
taught him how to sing
and dance. The first
song feast was so joyful
that animals became
human, and old eagles
became young again.

FOUR WHO TRAVELED AROUND THE WORLD

Two men decided to find out how big the world was, so each
man set off with his wife in opposite directions. They traveled
far across the ice with their dog sleds, carrying on year after year.
As they journeyed, their families grew, and eventually two tribes
formed. The two couples grew so old and frail that they had to ride
on their sleds rather than walk beside them. But their children and
grandchildren helped them, and the old people were able to carry on
their journey. One day, each of the travelers saw a group of people
and sleds coming toward them in the far distance. They had gone
all around the world and returned to their starting point. At
last they knew how big the world was – and then they died.

THE TWO MEN, NOW VERY OLD, MEET AFTER THEIR JOURNEY AROUND THE WORLD

MASK
REPRESENTING
A POLAR BEAR

MASK OF THE
MOON MAN,
IGALUK

*Hoops represent
levels of the
cosmos*

*Feather
signifies
a star*

*White border
around face
symbolizes air*

IGALUK

The Moon
Man Igaluk
once slept with
his sister by mistake.
When they discovered
what they had done,
they were so ashamed
that they left the
earth for ever. Igaluk
became the moon, and
his sister the sun. After
he had gone to the
sky, Igaluk looked
after the human race,
controlling the seasons
of the year and the
movement of the tides.

WANDER-HAWK

One of the Inuit heroes
is called Wander-hawk,
a man from the inland
woods. He settled by
the coast, becoming a
skilled hunter on land
and sea. He travels
around the world,
using his magic
powers to root out evil
wherever he finds it.

POLAR BEAR

The wife of a hunter had an affair with a polar bear. Her husband smelled
bear in the igloo and made his wife tell him where her lover lived. The
bear managed to escape when the hunter went to kill him. Angry that
the woman had given him away, the bear decided to crush the igloo
in revenge. But when he got there he forgave the woman and walked
away into the snow, beginning a long, solitary search for true love.

EASTERN NORTH AMERICA

THE VAST AREA OF EASTERN NORTH AMERICA is home to many peoples, living in diverse terrains – from the cool northeastern woodlands to the warm southeast. Popular mythological themes across the whole region include a belief in an Upper and Lower World, with the earth, or Middle World, in between; respect for the spiritual power of nature; and the idea that many beings can change from animal to human shape and back again.

GLOOSKAP RETURNS HOME AFTER DEFEATING EVIL SPIRITS

GLOOSKAP

The creator and trickster Glooskap, the principal hero of the Algonquin, made the sun, moon, plants, animals, and people from Mother Earth's body. Malsum, his wicked brother, created troublesome mountains, reptiles, and insects. A mighty warrior, Glooskap killed Malsum, who went to live in the underworld, and banished evil spirits from the earth, sending them to join Malsum. As a trickster, Glooskap could change shape, using his cunning to fight his opponents.

SKY HOLDER

The Iroquois creator, Sky Holder, sent two spirits to help the people on earth. He sent Ohswedogo to the west and Twehdaigo to the east. A separate spirit rebelled and challenged Sky Holder's power. In the resulting struggle, the spirit's face was injured and he became known as Old Broken Nose. He was condemned to wander the earth, curing people of their ills, and this is how he acquired his other name – Great Doctor.

MAIDEN MAKING A SACRIFICIAL PLUNGE OVER NIAGARA FALLS

HINON

The Seneca thunder spirit, Hinon, lives in a cave beneath Niagara Falls. He is known to care for people attacked by reptiles. Once a girl, in despair because a snake had invaded her body and killed her husband, decided to throw herself over the Falls in a canoe. Hinon rescued her and removed the snake. The girl stayed with Hinon for a while, then decided to return to her people.

Raven's beak

Bowl for tobacco

HOPEWELL CARVED STONE PIPE IN THE FORM OF A RAVEN

RAVEN

A myth of the trickster Raven tells how he brought fire to the world. Raven looked into the distance and saw smoke rising from the village of the Fire People. He went to the village with his friends – Robin, Mole, and Flea – and tried to steal their fire, but failed. Robin's feathers were scorched, so Mole burrowed underground to the chief's house, and Raven stole the chief's baby. He held it ransom, demanding fire in exchange for the child. The chief gave fire to the Raven, along with two stones to strike together to make a spark.

THE TWINS

Sky Woman's daughter had twin sons – Good Mind and Evil Mind. Good Mind made the earth a wonderful place in which to live, and created people from clay. Evil Mind made mischief. He hid the sun and destroyed the good things that his brother had made.

RATTLE MADE FROM A TURTLE SHELL

THE TRICKSTER LOX, AS A WOLVERINE

TURTLE ISLAND

A northeastern myth explains how Turtle told the diving creatures to go to the bottom of the sea and get some earth to put on his back. Many aquatic animals tried, but Muskrat was the only one who succeeded. When he put the soil on the Turtle's shell, it grew to form an island – the earth.

LOX

The trickster Lox takes the form of a wolverine, according to the Passamaquoddy people, and he is feared for both his strength and his cunning. Lox follows hunters, invades their camp, and destroys everything he can. Anything that cannot be broken, he carries away to hide.

ASPENS TREMBLE WHEN STRONG WIND BLOWS

STRONG WIND

The Micmac hero, Strong Wind, travels through the air in a sled drawn by the rainbow, and the Milky Way forms his bowstring. Strong Wind married a girl with a burned face but a loving heart. She had three wicked sisters, whom Strong Wind turned into aspens. These trees still tremble when Strong Wind comes near.

SPIRITS OF GOOD AND EVIL

The Lenape creator is called Welsit Manatu (Good Spirit). He made all things in the world: creating the earth from mud, forming humans, and growing useful plants for people to eat and to use as medicines. He also helped the people by killing or transforming harmful beings: for example, reducing the huge man-eating squirrel to a small size. His work is undone by the evil Mahtantu, who created poisonous plants and bats.

FEMALE SPIRIT DOLL OF THE DELAWARE

Wampum belt used in peace negotiations

W'AXKOK

The horned serpent W'axkok is a water monster who appears in tales of the Lenape. In one story, he bewitches a young woman and takes her for his wife. She does not realize that she is living underwater with the serpent until 12 women come to kill the monster, and a boy arrives to remove snake children from her womb.

THE SUN'S GRIEF

The Cherokee tell how the Sun's daughter died from a snake bite. The Sun wept and hid herself, causing flooding and darkness on earth. The mortals sent a group of young people to sing and dance for the Sun, which cheered her up. Once again the Sun smiled on the earth.

DEGANAWIDAH AND HIAWATHA

The five nations of the Iroquois people (Mohawk, Onondaga, Seneca, Oneida, and Cayuga) were continually at war. The prophet Deganawidah had a vision in which all the Iroquois were united. The Mohawk chief Hiawatha, renowned for his intelligence and trusted by all five tribes, was able to persuade the nations to unite.

STAR HUSBAND

Two Ojibwa girls married stars and found themselves in the heavens. They made a rope of roots to get back down to earth, but landed in an eagle's nest and had to be rescued by **Lox**.

Tobacco

Corn

WATER BEETLE

Cherokee myth tells how the creatures who lived in the Upper World began to run out of room. They sent Water Beetle to explore the watery Lower World. He brought back some mud and piled it into a mound to make the earth. The Buzzard flapped his wings over the mud to dry it out. When the Buzzard flew low over the earth, his wings scraped along the mud, creating mountains and valleys.

IMPORTANT CROPS CREATED BY THE FIRST MOTHER OF THE PENOBSCOT

FIRST MOTHER

When there was a great famine, the First Mother of the Penobscot people was very sad. She told her husband that he must kill her. At first he could not do this, and went to the Great Teacher for advice. He was told to do what his wife wished. She told him to drag her body around the field and bury her in the middle. In seven months there was enough tobacco and corn in the field for everyone to eat, and they saved some seeds to plant for next year's crop.

BEAR BROTHER

Once during a great famine, the Cherokee met to discuss what to do. One family left to live in the forest, where they turned into bears and were hunted by the rest of the people. Ever since, the hunter has said to his animal quarry, "Thank you, my brother."

RABBIT

The trickster Rabbit (or Hare) plays a similar role to the Raven in some cultures, by bringing fire to the people and playing many pranks. One story tells of Orphan Boy, who had a headdress made of rattlesnakes and blue jays. Rabbit stole the headdress and was punished by being thrown to the dogs. He escaped by putting the dogs to sleep.

TRICKSTER RABBIT

DAY AND NIGHT

Creek legend tells how the animals met to discuss how day and night should be divided. Some creatures wanted it always to be day, others wanted continuous night. Then Ground Squirrel said that the two should be equally divided – like the stripes on Raccoon's tail.

Stripes on Raccoon's tail represent day and night

THE GREAT PLAINS

THE PEOPLES OF THE GREAT PLAINS of the United States began as nomadic hunters whose quarry was the buffalo. Their culture began to flourish during the 18th century, when the horse was introduced to the area, enabling tribes to travel with ease across the wide open grasslands and over rivers and streams. The buffalo gave the Plains people everything, from food to coverings for their tepees, so it is not surprising that this animal plays a major role in Plains mythology. But the traditional stories of the Plains involve many different animals, from the coyote to the beaver. Human heroes could often take animal form, and Plains animal stories reflect the deep spiritual power that the shamans, or medicine men, held over the natural world. Many ceremonies involved people coming together to experience or use this power for a variety of purposes: to help encourage the hunters, to heal the sick, or to foster good relations between tribes.

Protective buffalo symbol

SHIELD OF A PLAINS WARRIOR

VISION QUEST
A young man from the Plains was expected to go on a vision quest before coming of age. He would retire to some remote or sacred place, where he hoped to have a vision that would give him some of the power that belonged to the spirits of the natural world around him.

CORN WOMAN AND BUFFALO WOMAN
The Pawnee tell how a hunter called Without Wings had two wives. They were Buffalo Woman, from the east, who caused the buffalo herds to scatter, and Corn Woman, from the west, who made the corn grow. Buffalo Woman's daughter fought with Corn Woman's son, and the two women parted company. Corn Woman went to live underground, while Buffalo Woman joined her herds.

Thunderbird design

GHOST DANCE shirt

Lone Man tells the people that the totem pole will protect them once he has gone

GHOST DANCE
Some Plains peoples believe that one day their dead will return to earth, and it will become a paradise where people live for ever. A special dance – the Ghost Dance – was performed to prepare for this resurrection. It was done for long stretches with little rest. Dancers decorated their skin with black, white, and red paint.

OLD MAN COYOTE
Coyote is a popular hero of peoples such as the Crow, who were sad that they had no summer. Woman with the Strong Heart kept summer and winter in different bags. Coyote went to her tepee and stole the bag containing summer. Finally, an agreement was reached so that each land should have its fair share of winter and summer.

LODGE-BOY AND THROWN-AWAY
The twins Lodge-boy and Thrown-away were taken from their mother's womb when she died. They became famous heroes, always daring to rid the world of dangers. They killed a deadly alligator, slew vicious snakes, and caught an otter that was eating the **Thunderbird**'s young.

BUFFALO DANCE
The buffalo was a source of meat, hide for clothes and shelters, and bone to make tools. The Plains hunters understood that it was vital to perform the right ceremonies to make the hunt successful. These included rituals to call the buffalo, and dances after the hunt, when the beast's head was displayed on top of a pole.

FIRST CREATOR
In the beginning, this world was all water. First Creator and **Lone Man** were walking on the water when they saw a mud hen diving down. The bird seemed to go deep below the surface. First Creator and Lone Man told it to dive down again and fetch sand from the bottom, from which they made the earth. First Creator made the hilly country, and Lone Man, the flat. Later, First Creator turned into **Coyote**.

LONE MAN
The Mandans ascended to this world from one below. They climbed up a grapevine, but one pregnant woman was too heavy and the vine broke, trapping half of them below. They brought corn with them, and one of their first chiefs, Good Furred Robe, taught them songs to make the corn grow. Lone Man turned himself into a corncob and caused a young Mandan woman to eat it. She bore a child who became a great teacher and guide of the Mandan nation.

WAKAN-TANKA

The Lakota believe that a vast creative power called Wakan-Tanka (Great Mystery) exists in the universe. All the great forces in nature, from crashing thunder to the rainbow's bright colors, were caused by Wakan-Tanka. **Shamans** try to harness Wakan-Tanka to do good in the world.

TIRAWA

The supreme god of the Pawnee, Tirawa is present in all things, especially thunder. Its noise is said to be the sound of the gods returning to earth after winter's end. Tirawa created the first man and woman, showed them how to live, and how to make the first altar with the skull of a buffalo.

SACRED THUNDER MEDICINE PIPE

Eagle feathers

PTESAN WIN

White Buffalo Calf Woman, or Ptesan Win, brought the first sacred pipe to the Lakotas. It was carved with a buffalo calf and adorned with eagle feathers. After showing them how to use it, she changed into a white buffalo.

DECORATED BUFFALO SKULL, USED IN THE SUN DANCE

PIPE DEPICTING SPIRITS OF A MAN, A WOMAN, AND A HORSE

SACRED PIPE

Pipes were traditionally seen as sacred objects. In many tribes, they were given to the people at the time of creation by an animal spirit such as Bear or White Buffalo Maiden. Ceremonies are often opened with ritual pipe smoking, and the pipe is used during important rituals such as the **Sun Dance**.

FALLING STAR

Many stories tell of a young woman who falls in love with a star. Their child, Falling Star, becomes a hero. In the Cheyenne version, he slew a great water monster that devoured people. But his greatest deed was to kill the white crow that flew after the buffalo, warning them when hunters were near.

BUFFALO EFFIGY

SUN DANCE

The Sun Dance is part of an annual ritual, celebrating the sun's part in creating the universe and ensuring the annual renewal of the world. A pole is set up, linking the worlds above and below the earth. People gather in a circle – those wanting to absorb the sun's spiritual and creative power dance around the pole. People may dance for days, finally going into a trance or collapsing from exhaustion. Their physical sufferings are undergone as offerings to the Great Spirit.

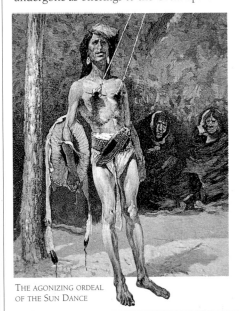

THE AGONIZING ORDEAL OF THE SUN DANCE

Turtle represents Earth Diver

DETAIL OF A CHEYENNE SHIELD

EARTH DIVER

The Earth Diver takes part in many North American creation myths, taking the form of a beaver, beetle, duck, mink, or turtle. In the beginning, water stretched across the world. The Earth Diver swam to the bottom of the water and brought some mud to the surface, which the creator used to make the earth. In some accounts, **Old Man Coyote** tells the Earth Diver to collect the mud.

GREAT BEAVER

According to the Cheyenne, the Upper and Lower Worlds are separated by a long wooden pole. The North's Great White Grandfather Beaver is continually chewing at this pole. It is said that if he chews all the way through, the heavens will collapse onto the earth, bringing about the end of the world.

SEE ALSO

WEST COAST

THE WEST COAST OF NORTH AMERICA is home to many very different peoples, from the salmon fishers of the northwestern forest's rivers and lakes to the desert tribes of arid southern California. The people of the Northwest developed an elaborate cult of their ancestors. Each tribe had its own animal ancestors, whose figures were carved on totem poles erected outside their houses. The many animals in their mythology include the trickster Raven and the fearsome and gigantic Thunderbird. Their creation stories often involve an Upper World, which fits over earth like an enormous bowl, and deities who can transform their shape into many unusual and terrifying beings.

TOBACCO PIPE SHOWING THE TRICKSTER RAVEN WITH A FISHERMAN'S WIFE

RAVEN
For many northwestern tribes, Raven helped the creator finish the job of making the world; gifts such as berries come from him. Raven turned himself into a pine needle, which was swallowed by the Sky Chief's daughter. As a result, she had a son, to whom the Sky Chief gave a box with the sun inside. The child transformed back into Raven, left heaven, and flew across the sky, opening the box periodically to produce daylight.

BRIGHT CLOUD WOMAN
Raven's wife on earth is a salmon-woman known as Bright Cloud Woman. Like Raven, she can change her shape, and she can leave the river. But she usually lives in her own kingdom under the water, where she and the other fish can take human form. Bright Cloud Woman is protectress of fish, especially salmon, but every year her charges offer their flesh to the human fishermen.

TRANSFORMATION MASK

Bird's head painted inside mask

Image representing spirit of clan ancestor

Head with human features, except for bird's beak

KWATYAT
Among the Nootkas, Kwatyat is both hero and trickster who can transform himself into any shape. He is said to be the creator, responsible for making everything in the Nootka cosmos. He had many adventures – turning a pool of grease into a lake, stealing land from a wolf chief, and exploding through sweating too much. Finally, he vanished toward the south and took a river with him.

String for opening and closing mask

SALMON RATTLE CONTAINING AN EFFIGY OF A SHAMAN

Carved face representing the Spirit of the sun

HAIDA TOTEM POLE

WAKIASH
The Northwest coast peoples make totem poles to represent their ancestors. Once a chief called Wakiash was upset because he did not have a dance of his own. He flew around the world with **Raven**, and they came upon a house with a totem pole outside. Inside were dancing animals. Wakiash liked the house so much that he put it in his bundle and took it home with him. When he threw down the bundle, the house and pole re-appeared. Inspired by the animals, Wakiash copied their dance. As he danced, the house and pole vanished, but Wakiash carved his own totem pole – the first in his tribe.

WOMAN WHO MARRIED THE SUN
The Bella Coola people believe that the sun took a human wife. When her son was born, she slid back down to earth on the sun's eyelashes, or sunbeams. On earth, her son was teased because he did not have a father, so he shot a chain of arrows into the sky and climbed up them to the sun. He wanted to take his father's place. But he was too hasty, and lit all the sun's torches together to produce a blistering heat. The result was disaster on earth – the trees burned, water boiled, and many animals, who could not find any shade in which to hide, had their coats scorched black. The sun cast him out of the sky, and he landed on earth. Here he became the Mink – the trickster of many of the West Coast peoples – destined to be hunted forever.

BELLA COOLA SUN MASK

BEAR MOTHER

The Haida people tell a story about a woman, Kind-a-wuss, who was not allowed to marry her beloved, Quiss-an-kweedas, because they belonged to the same family. Instead, she went to live with the chief of the bears. The bear chief was kind to her, and the couple had two sons, but eventually Quiss-an-kweedas found her. The people allowed the human couple to marry, out of pity for the hardship they had suffered.

Hands feature faces of Bear mother's two cubs

POTLATCH

In the Northwest, the true sign of a chief's status is his ability to give away his wealth. The people organize lavish ceremonies – called potlatches – where the chief hands out gifts to hundreds of guests, who have come from all over the region. The chief does not lose his wealth, because being a giver at one potlatch means that you will be given gifts at all the others.

Engraved copper, highly prized as a potlatch gift

Carved wooden beaver on Haida headdress

THE WAR OF BEAVER AND PORCUPINE

Beaver and Porcupine started out as good friends, but one day, Porcupine stole Beaver's food, so Beaver played a trick on him. Beaver offered to give Porcupine a ride on his back, but left him on a stump in the middle of a lake. Porcupine conjured up cold weather to freeze the lake so he could return to Beaver. Then he decided that he would get back at his former friend. This time, Porcupine offered Beaver a ride, and left Beaver stranded at the top of a very tall tree. Beaver could not climb down, but figured out how to gnaw his way down to the ground. Ever since, beavers have been experts at cutting wood.

WOOD CARVING OF THUNDERBIRD, MYTHICAL CREATURE OF THE HAIDA

THUNDERBIRDS

Feared all over North America, the Thunderbird is like an enormous eagle that can swoop down from the sky and carry away any living creature – even something as enormous as a whale. The flash when he blinks his eyes makes lightning, and the thunder is caused by the beating of his wings. Sometimes he travels around with a pair of lightning serpents, which are said to transform themselves into his belt and his harpoon. Although the bird is dangerous, with the power to cause rapid death, many people believe that seeing or hearing the Thunderbird is a sign of good luck or forthcoming wealth.

CALIFORNIA

The native peoples of California make up a distinct culture group. The area has many separate tribes, with a variety of myths. Most have a creation story that begins with the world covered in water. In some places, the trickster Coyote helps the creator bring the earth into being.

LIZARD-HAND

Most cultures have a myth that explains the origins of death. One such myth from California involves **Coyote**. The creatures were discussing what form humans should take – Coyote wanted the hands of humans to be closed fists, like his own, but Lizard disagreed, insisting that people must have open hands with five fingers, like Lizard himself. Coyote reluctantly agreed, but humans had to pay a price for their useful hands. "Well then," Coyote decided, "They will have to die."

LIZARD-SHAPED PENDANT AS A GOOD LUCK CHARM

KUMUSH

Known as the Old Man of the Ancients, Kumush is the creator god of the Modoc tribe. He made the land of the Modoc and told the rivers and hills to care for the people. Kumush went to the house of death after his daughter died, and returned with a bag of bones, which he planted in the ground. From these bones, the Modoc people were created.

COYOTE

The trickster Coyote had a son whom he loved dearly. One day, the boy went to the river to get some water. The rushes turned into rattlesnakes and killed the boy. Coyote was grief-stricken. He realized that bringing death was a bad idea, and pleaded with the creator, Earthmaker, to bring the boy back to life. When Earthmaker refused, Coyote became an everlasting mischief-maker in the world.

COYOTE, THE ETERNAL MISCHIEF-MAKER

White eagle feather

Magpie tail feather

Swansdown represents an eagle

TLINGIT SHAMAN'S HEADDRESS

TLINGIT SPIRITS

Like most Native American peoples, the Tlingit believe that the natural world is full of animal spirits. Each, even the mosquito, has its own origin story. A giant preyed on humans, biting their flesh and drinking their blood. But a hero killed the giant, chopping him up and burning the pieces. From these ashes arose the first cloud of mosquitoes.

SEE ALSO

RAVEN 98 • COYOTE 100

CREATION MYTHS 8
GODS AND GODDESSES 10
HEROES AND TRICKSTERS 12
MYTHICAL MONSTERS 14
ANIMALS AND PLANTS 16
ENDINGS 18

SOUTHWEST

THE SOUTHWESTERN REGION of the United States is a unique land of dry deserts and cold mountains. It is home to the Pueblo peoples who settled here more than 2,000 years ago. They built their stone or mud-brick villages called pueblos on tabletop rocks known as mesas or along the few rivers, and began to grow corn. The Navaho and Apache peoples, who also live in the area, migrated from the Northwest about 600 years ago. These two peoples began as hunters and warriors, but they took up farming and adopted a more settled, agricultural life in the Southwest. In this arid region, water is one of the most valuable resources and the mythology of the Southwest features many spirits who are bringers of rain. Southwestern peoples also share similar emergence myths, in which people appear on earth after passing through a series of different worlds.

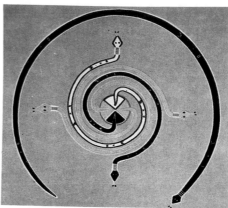

NAVAHO SAND PAINTING

SAND PAINTINGS
Using clean sand mixed with colored charcoal and pollen, Navaho sand paintings show stylized scenes from their mythology. During curing ceremonies, called Chantways, the priests ask for the gods' help, to produce bountiful harvests or to heal the sick. The paintings are made according to set patterns, and every detail must be correct.

Corn plant flanked by two holy people

NAVAHO BLANKET BASED ON A SAND PAINTING DESIGN

CHANGING WOMAN
The Navaho's supreme creator god made Changing Woman, the creator goddess, from a piece of turquoise. She created people, using a mixture of corn dust and skin from her breasts. Changing Woman lives on an island in the west, from which she sends fresh breezes and life-giving rains to water the lands of the Navaho. Changing Woman represents nature and birth, growing old and then young again, in a continuing cycle.

Changing Woman grows old in winter and young again in summer

TWINS
Many southwestern peoples tell of twin brothers, who are the sun's children and heroes. Their victories are thought to bring good fortune to the people. At times they are seen as war gods, but in their gentler guise, they are called the Beloved Two.

SKY BOY
The Apache Creator thought the cosmos into existence, and sang the sky into being. At the first sweat lodge he created three people – Sky Boy, chief sky god; Earth Daughter, goddess of the earth and crops; and Pollen Girl, goddess of human health and medicine.

GIRL WITHOUT PARENTS
The first living being made by the Apache Creator was Girl Without Parents, who appeared sitting on a floating cloud. She helped create the world by kicking a small ball made by the Creator until it became the vast earth.

CORN BOY AND CORN GIRL
White Corn Boy and Yellow Corn Girl, made from two ears of corn by the Navaho's Creator god, brought corn to the Navaho, and it became their main food source. Corn is the Navaho's sacred plant, and is used in religious ceremonies. Masks worn by **shamans** are fed cornmeal to "bring them to life."

SUN GOD
Tsohanoai, the Navaho sun god, is the primal Creator and **Changing Woman**'s husband. Each day he carries the sun on his back across the sky, before hanging it up on the western wall of his house at night. Tsohanoai and Changing Woman had two sons – Killer of Enemies and Child of Water. At first, the sun god would not acknowledge his sons and threw them out when the pair hid in his house. But later he gave them magic arrows to fight the world's evil spirits.

Tsohanoai

As Tsohanoai shakes the rug, Killer of Enemies and Child of Water fall out

SNAKE DANCE

For the Hopi and Zuni, the snake is a symbol of fertility. A Hopi story tells how the young hero Tiyo became a member of the Snake Clan, married Snake Maiden, and taught his people the dance. The Snake Dance is still performed as a rain-making ceremony in which snakes, said to carry the peoples' prayers for rain, are caught and made members of the Snake Society. During the dance itself, priests hold snake-shaped sticks and carry live rattlesnakes in their mouths.

ZUNI AND HOPI SNAKE, SYMBOL OF FERTILITY

Feathers are a typical decoration

PAINTED WOODEN KACHINA DOLL

SUN FATHER

Sun Father and his wife Moonlight-Giving Mother, known as the Ones Who Hold Our Roads, are two of the most important Raw People. They are Zuni spirits who can take human form, but can also transform themselves; ordinary humans are Cooked People. Sun Father's sons, the hero twins, rid the world of monsters and learned how to make rain.

A god and spirits painted on warrior's cloak

THE EMERGENCE

The origin of the southwestern peoples is told in terms of several different worlds, which are layered one above the other. If one world is no longer suitable for humans (because of floods or its small size), people climb up from that world, to emerge into the next. People are helped in different ways, such as climbing up a reed or a fir tree, to emerge through a hole made by a woodpecker. Emergence stories are most sacred and must never be told to strangers or children.

KACHINAS

According to the Hopi, when good people die, their spirits become kachinas. These spirits look after the interests of all humankind, passing on humans' messages to the gods and then bringing back to the people good fortune in the shape of fertility, power, and long life. But in the dry Southwest, one quality of kachinas is valued above all others – the ability to bring rain.

Turquoise eye

FROG MADE OF JET AND TURQUOISE

FROG

One of the myths of the Diegueños people tells how an enraged Frog made death come into the world. People laughed at Frog because of his odd shape and nakedness, so Frog became angry at the Creator. In his rage, Frog spat poison into the Creator's drinking water. When the creator god realized what had happened, he knew that he would die. Because all things on earth were the Creator's children, every living thing also had to die eventually.

WOVEN BLANKET WITH HUNTING MOTIFS

SPIDER WOMAN

This Hopi spirit, known as Spider Woman or Grandma, appears as a spider or as an old woman, but is welcome in either form because she brings good fortune. She helps those in peril or advises on healing the sick; she also teaches weaving. Her kind spirit is revered by the Hopi and other peoples of the Southwest for her great power and her ability to solve problems.

GREAT BUTTERFLY

Butterflies play important roles in the mythology of the Southwest. For the Zuni, butterflies were created when a **kachina** called Paiyatemu played the flute. In Navaho myth, they appeared when a hero used a butterfly disguise. The Pima tell how the creator spirit Cherwit Maké (Great Butterfly) fluttered down from the clouds to the Blue Cliffs, where the Verde and Salt Rivers meet. Here he created humans from his own sweat.

ELDER BROTHER

Elder Brother, a Pima spirit, destroyed the world in a flood and created a new race of people. Angry at this, the Creator sent Elder Brother's people to the underworld. Buzzard killed Elder Brother, who came back to life to rescue his people.

MAYA

THE POWERFUL CIVILIZATION of the Maya people flourished in Mexico between AD 250 and 900. Maya culture was based around ceremonial centers with large plazas and pyramid-temples where they worshiped their gods. The Maya recorded the stories of their gods using their own special picture-writing. About 30 deities are mentioned, but there were many more, often taking human or animal form. Many Maya gods presided over the weather and crops, both of which were vital if the Maya were to produce enough food to survive and prosper.

KINICH-AHAU
The Ancient Maya sun god was Kinich-Ahau, the Lord of the Face of the Sun. Like many sun gods, he had different identities in the day and night. During the daytime, as he traveled across the sky, Kinich-Ahau could appear in either young or old forms, but he is usually portrayed with a large Roman nose. But during the hours of darkness, on his nightly journey through the underworld, he transformed into the **Jaguar God**.

EAGLE
The harpy eagle was a symbol of time, and so was associated with the sun god **Kinich-Ahau**, who marked day from night when he passed through the sky. The eagle stood for the "katun," a division of the complex Maya calendar lasting 7,200 days. Each Maya "year" equaled 360 days.

Itzamna holding a vision serpent

JAGUAR GOD

Tears shed by Chac brought gentle rains to earth

ITZAMNA
The creator Itzamna, lord of the heavens and god of day and night, is one of the most important Maya deities. In spite of his high status, his appearance was unimpressive – he was portrayed as a toothless old man with a hooked nose. Itzamna helped humankind with his healing powers. The Maya believed that he was the inventor of writing and the creator of their religious rituals.

Snake

IXCHEL
Itzamna's wife Ixchel (Lady Rainbow) was an old woman with great power. Goddess of pregnancy, midwifery, childbirth, and fertility, Ixchel also looked after weavers and was able to foretell the future. Maya women went on long pilgrimages to pray at her temples.

JAGUAR GOD
The jaguar, the largest and most powerful of the Central American cats, was admired and feared by the earliest peoples of Mexico and is one of the oldest gods of the region. The Maya Jaguar God was, therefore, a terrifying deity of darkness, who ruled the underworld (called Xibalba). He was also a symbol of power, kingship, and the earth's fertility. Priests who dressed in jaguar skins brought these qualities to life in ceremonies designed to heal the sick or bring success to hunting expeditions.

CHAC
The Maya rain god Chac was portrayed as a weeping warrior whose tears rained down on the earth. Unlike the fearsome **Ixchel**, Chac was a friendly figure who brought gentle rain to water farmers' fields. He was sacred to everyone who grew food, and became god of agriculture. According to one story, he brought maize (Indian corn) to the Maya people, by opening a stone in which the first maize plant was hidden. He was often worshiped as four separate, but beneficial, gods, each of a different color – one for each of the points of the compass.

RAIN GOD CHAC

AH PUCH

With his exposed bones and skull-like head, the grim god of death Ah Puch was unmistakable. In the Maya texts, his symbols were also easy to recognize – a skull and the head of a corpse. Ah Puch was widely feared by the Maya. He was said to visit the houses of the sick and dying, ready to snatch away their souls and take them to Mitnal, the kingdom of the dead in the west.

Corpselike head of Ah Puch, god of death

TOHIL

The god of fire and sacrifice was Tohil. According to the Maya creation legend, the first age of the world came to an end when fire and flood destroyed the world. At the beginning of the second age, the ancestors of the people emerged in a place called Seven Caves, where they met Tohil for the first time.

Necklace signifying power

VUCUB CAQUIX

The monstrous vulture Vucub Caquix was the sun god of the previous age of the universe. This giant figure had two powerful sons – Earthquake and Earth Heaper. A terrifying monster, Vucub Caquix caused destruction and unhappiness in the world, and was finally destroyed by the hero twins.

STORM GODDESS

The Maya storm goddess is sometimes said to be one of the incarnations of **Ixchel**. Her power to work with the sky serpent to create floods was greatly feared. Downpours were a result of her anger with people on earth. The priests of the storm goddess tried to calm her with frequent sacrifices. Her fearsome images show her with a snake on her head and crossbones on her clothes.

PAUAHTUN

A god with four separate incarnations, Pauahtun stood at the four corners of the heavens, holding up the sky and the upper realm, which the Maya believed to exist above the world. In spite of this important job, Pauahtun was a drunkard. He was also an unpredictable god of thunder and wind. His symbols were the shells of the tortoise and conch, which he is often shown holding.

BALL GAME

The hero twins **Xbalanque** and **Hunahpu** made a pounding noise when they played the Maya ritual ball game. This annoyed the gods, who demanded that the twins go to the underworld. They successfully underwent a series of trials until a killer bat removed Hunahpu's head. The death gods threw his head into their ball court to be used as a ball, but Xbalanque hit it out of the court. The gods were distracted, thinking that a passing rabbit was the ball. Xbalanque was able to put the head back on his brother's neck. After their deaths, the twins were reborn as the sun and moon.

Clothing padded to protect player

BALLPLAYER IN ACTION

HUN HUNAHPU

The father of the hero twins was the maize god Hun Hunahpu. The most famous story about Hun Hunahpu concerns his death. He and his brother were challenged to a **ball game** in the realm of the dead, but when they arrived there, they were mercilessly put to death by the rulers of the underworld. It was left to his sons – the hero twins – to avenge Hun Hunahpu's death.

HUNAHPU AND XBALANQUE

The twin brothers Hunahpu and Xbalanque were the culture heroes of the Quiche Maya. Famous for their **ball game** with the gods in the underworld, they also showed them how they could be cut into pieces and repair themselves. The gods were impressed and asked for this to be done to them. The twins tricked the gods, cutting them up but refusing to repair them.

Corncob sprouting from Hun Hunahpu's head

HUN BATZ AND HUN CHOUEN

Hun Hunahpu's elder sons, Hun Batz and Hun Chouen, were trained dancers and artists, relying on their younger brothers, the hero twins, to hunt. **Xbalanque** and **Hunahpu** resented this, and tricked Hun Batz and Hun Chouen into climbing a tree. It magically began to grow and they were stuck. The twins turned them into monkeys, so they could climb down – which is why monkeys became the protectors of artists and dancers.

AZTEC

THE AZTECS HAD A POWERFUL EMPIRE in Mexico by the 15th century. Their capital was at Tenochtitlan (modern Mexico City) on a swampy island in Lake Texcoco. According to legend, they arrived there after a long journey to find an eagle, symbol of the god Huitzilopochtli, perched on a large cactus with red fruit. The god told them to found their city here, at Tenochtitlan (Place of the Cactus Fruit). The Aztecs' rich culture was influenced by their predecessors, the Maya. Aztec pyramidal temples, ball game, and their use of human sacrifice in religious rituals were all features of Maya culture. The Aztecs also borrowed many of the Maya gods.

TEZCATLIPOCA
The foremost Aztec creator god was Tezcatlipoca (Lord of the Smoking Mirror). His magic mirror enabled him to predict the future. Tezcatlipoca took many forms and all the other creator gods were said to be incarnations of him. He was also called Yoalli Ehecatl and Tepeyollotli. In the latter form, he took the shape of the jaguar, the Aztec king of the beasts.

MASK OF TEZCATLIPOCA

Flayed skin of sacrificial victim

XIPE TOTEC, GOD OF SPRINGTIME

THE FEATHERED SERPENT, QUETZALCOATL

QUETZALCOATL
Child of the earth and the sun, the serpent Quetzalcoatl was the god of the spirit of life and of the wind. His name means both Feathered Serpent and Precious Twin. Worshiped as the god of priests and of learning, he was said to have invented the calendar. The Aztecs believed that they lived in the Fifth Sun, or Era, of the earth. Each of the previous Suns ended with a catastrophe. After the first four Suns, Quetzalcoatl went with **Xolotl** to the underworld and stole the bones with which to make the people of the Fifth Sun.

Symbols of the planets

XOLOTL, THE DESTRUCTIVE TWIN OF QUETZALCOATL

Patch over burst eye

Axe

CHALCHIUHTLICUE
Goddess of rivers, springs, and lakes, Chalchiuhtlicue could cause whirlwinds and hurricanes. Her name means Jade Skirt. She was the wife of the rain god **Tlaloc**. Chalchiuhtlicue was also worshiped as a goddess of childbirth and protector of children because of the water that breaks before a woman gives birth.

MASK OF CHALCHIUHTLICUE

TLALOC, GOD OF RAIN AND FERTILITY

XOLOTL
Quetzalcoatl had a twin brother, Xolotl, who took the form of a deformed dog. When people prayed to Xolotl, his response depended on the way his ears were pointing. He helped create humanity but his unpredictable nature made him resent his own creation, causing him to bring people misfortune. As a symbol of the hardships he had endured he had a burst eye. He was worshiped as god of the **ball game** and twins.

XIPE TOTEC
The god of plants and of springtime, Xipe Totec was one of four Aztec creator gods. His name means Flayed Lord, because at his festivals, victims were sacrificed and flayed (skinned alive). The skins were worn by priests, until they rotted and fell off. The disappearance of the old skin was a symbol of new life in spring.

TLALOC
Fertility and rain god, Tlaloc made the soil fertile, but was also capable of causing violent thunderstorms. Tlaloc presided over a whole army of gods and goddesses, some linked to corn-growing, and a troop of deities known as the 400 rabbits. Young children were sacrificed at his mountaintop festivals.

OMETEOTL

The supreme creator in Aztec mythology, Ometeotl lived in the highest part of heaven, Omeyocan (Place of Duality). Ometeotl took various forms, including a dual incarnation: male Ometecuhtli and female Omecihuatl. This primal couple produced the four great Aztec creator gods – **Tezcatlipoca**, **Huitzilopochtli**, **Xipe Totec**, and **Quetzalcoatl**.

OMETEOTL IN THE MALE INCARNATION OF OMETECUHTLI

SCULPTURE OF COYOLXAUHQUI

Golden bells make the moon glow

MICTLANTECUHTLI

Pleated conical cap

Skull symbolizing death

Double corncob

CHICOMECOATL

COYOLXAUHQUI

The ancient goddess of the moon and daughter of the earth goddess Coatlicue, Coyolxauhqui, or Golden Bells, is named after the tiny bells she wore on her cheeks. She was killed by her brother **Huitzilopochtli**, who, as soon as he was born, cut off Coyolxauhqui's head and hurled it into the sky, where it became the moon.

MICTLANTECUHTLI

The kingdom of the dead was known as Mictlan, and its ruler was Mictlantecuhtli, the god of death. To reach the peaceful and silent world of Mictlan, the soul of the dead person had to make a perilous journey through eight dark forests, across eight deserts, over eight mountains, and across a dangerous, fast-flowing river.

CORN GODDESS

The Aztecs had several deities who presided over the all-important corn crop. Two of these were Chicomecoatl, who represented the good seed corn that was stowed away for sowing next year, and Cinteotl, who could have both male and female forms. Springtime sacrifices to the corn deities ensured a good crop later in the year.

HUITZILOPOCHTLI

The Aztec war god Huitzilopochtli was identified with the sun and was said to be reborn every day. His name meant "blue hummingbird on the left" because it was thought dead warriors became hummingbirds, who flew to the underworld on the left.

XOCHIQUETZAL

Goddess of flowers, fruit, and music, Xochiquetzal (Most Precious Flower) was a bringer of human fertility, but ruled a part of the underworld set aside for warriors killed in battle and women who died giving birth to boys. At festivals she was given offerings of marigolds.

HUMAN SACRIFICE

The Aztecs believed that without the nourishment of human flesh and blood, the gods would not survive and the order of the universe would be destroyed, bringing about the end of civilization. So the Aztecs killed many people – often prisoners of war taken especially for sacrifice – on the altars of their temples. Many temples feature reclining statues of the Chacmool, or ritual attendant.

CHACMOOL

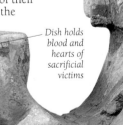

Dish holds blood and hearts of sacrificial victims

HUEHUETEOTL

The origins of the fire god, Huehueteotl, date back to the civilization of the Olmecs, which flourished in Mexico over 2,000 years before the Aztecs. For this reason, he was worshiped as the oldest Aztec god. Huehueteotl was usually portrayed as a toothless old man with a brazier on his head. His connection with fire and the hearth made him a popular household god.

SEE ALSO

BALL GAME 107
INCA 110 • MAYA 106

CREATION MYTHS 8
GODS AND GODDESSES 12

INCA

THE INCA EMPIRE was one of a series of South American civilizations based in the Andes mountains, and it extended along the Pacific coast from the northern part of present-day Ecuador through Peru to central Chile in the south. The Incas flourished in the 15th and early 16th centuries. They were sun worshipers, but had a number of other gods and goddesses, including an earth mother, a moon goddess, and many deities linked with weather, water, fertility, farming, and the heavens. The Inca civilization was famed for its skilled gold workers and stone masons, and its vast road system that united the difficult and mountainous region. But the civilization came to a sudden end in 1532, when explorers arrived from Spain and began to conquer much of South America.

Weeping God design on the Gateway of the Sun at Tiahuanaco

GOLD MASK OF INTI, THE SUN GOD

VIRACOCHA, THE SUPREME CREATOR GOD

INTI
The most important Inca god was Inti, the sun god. After the creation, Inti sent his son Manco Capac to earth, to be king and to teach people the arts of civilization. All later Inca rulers claimed to be Manco Capac's descendants, and were worshiped as part of the family of the sun god himself. Inti was worshiped at a huge temple of the sun in the Inca capital of Cuzco, Peru, where the mummies of emperors were placed when they died. The walls of the temple were lined with gold, which Incas believed was the sweat of the sun. When solar eclipses occurred, the Incas thought Inti was angry.

MAMA KILYA
The sister and wife of **Inti** was the moon goddess, Mama Kilya. She was the goddess of fertility, a witness of marriage vows, and the protector of women. With her different phases, Mama Kilya was also associated with the passing of time. The Incas were very superstitious about lunar eclipses. They believed that this showed Mama Kilya was being attacked by a massive snake. During eclipses, they would create as loud a noise as they could to frighten the serpent away.

WEEPING GOD
Before the Incas established their empire, there was a flourishing civilization at Tiahuanaco, Bolivia. Like the Incas, these people worshiped the sun god. A huge stone temple doorway – the Gateway of the Sun – is one of their most famous monuments. Little is known of their myths, but two stories of their origins say that the people came from a lake or a fountain, either of which could be represented by the tears streaming from the god's eyes, so their creator figure became the Weeping God.

VIRACOCHA
The supreme creator god, Viracocha, made the world and filled it with a race of giants. When these creatures disobeyed Viracocha, he destroyed them in a flood. At first, Viracocha brought light to the world by making the sun and moon rise from Lake Titicaca, Bolivia. Then he made humans from clay and left them in caves, from which they emerged onto the earth's surface. He then traveled the world, creating various landscape features before he sailed away.

PACHA MAMA
The earth goddess, Pacha Mama, was widely worshiped by the Incas. She was second only to the sun god **Inti**, because she was a giver of life to everything on earth. When the Incas first arrived at Cuzco, the inflated lungs of a llama were raised above the city as a symbol of the goddess. After that, llamas were often sacrificed to Pacha Mama. Another form of sacrifice was to offer the earth goddess coca leaves, to ensure that the fields would produce good crops, or to bring luck when building a new house.

CHUICHU

The god Chuichu was the Inca rainbow deity. He was an attendant both of **Inti** and **Mama Kilya**. The Incas depended heavily on both the rain and the sun for the success of their crops. A god who appeared when rain and sun came together, such as Chuichu, was especially powerful.

ILYAP'A

The thunder god Ilyap'a carried a sling, which he fired at a large pot of water. The sound of the sling produced thunder, lightning was made by the slingshot as it flew through the sky, and splashing water from the pot became rain. Ilyap'a was widely feared because sometimes children were sacrificed to him.

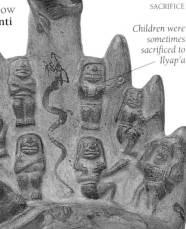

MOUNTAINTOP SACRIFICE

Children were sometimes sacrificed to Ilyap'a

STAR DEITIES

When Viracocha caused the sun and moon to appear, stars were also thrown up into the sky from Lake Titicaca. The Incas gave many stars and constellations the status of gods, and interpreted the patterns made by the some of the stars as animals – such as Yacana (the Llama).

ORQO-CILAY
This star group, known as the Llama of Many Colors, protected imperial llama flocks.

CHASKA-QOYLOR
The planet Venus or morning star was called Chaska-Qoylor (the Shaggy Star). Thought to be the sun's handmaiden, this planet was said to be a patron of princesses and other young girls.

THE PLEIADES
This group of stars was known as Collca (the Granary). They were worshiped as bringers of fertility. The Incas would watch the setting Pleiades around April 15 each spring.

MAMA COCHA
The goddess of the sea, water, and rain was Mama Cocha, a prominent figure in the Inca religion. She was the sister and wife of the creator **Viracocha**, who was also said to be a water deity.

THE EMERGENCE
Inca myths tell how the first people emerged from three cave mouths at a place called Paccari-tambo, near Cuzco. The divine ancestors of the Inca emperors emerged from the central cave, while mortal families appeared from the other two cave mouths. They made their way toward the site of Cuzco, looking for good land to settle, and eventually they founded the city.

LLAMA
The llama plays a key part in the Inca flood story. A man was taking a llama to pasture, but the creature would not eat and said that there would soon be a terrible flood. It told the farmer to climb a high mountain. Soon the waters rose, and the farmer was the only human to survive.

Moon headdress perhaps representing Mama Kilya

Corncob

Squash

INCAN AGRICULTURAL DEITY DECORATED WITH CORN AND SQUASHES

LLAMA, PART OF THE INCA FLOOD STORY

EL DORADO

The name *El Dorado* means The Golden Man. There was a story among the Spanish conquerors of South America that there was a land so rich that the king's body was adorned with gold dust. The story came from a real ritual that took place in the highlands of Colombia, where a new king had his body smeared with resin before being covered in gold dust. Such stories made the Spanish eager to conquer and plunder South America.

A GOLDEN RAFT WAS PART OF THE EL DORADO CEREMONY

HUACAS
Many natural features (called *huacas*), such as caves, trees, or springs, were said to have their own spirits. These spirits belonged to a more ancient religion than the other Inca gods, but were still worshiped alongside **Inti** and his family.

SEE ALSO

AFRICA

People have lived in Africa longer than in any other part of the world. Over many thousands of years, they spread across the continent, some living by hunting and gathering, and others by developing agriculture.

MYTHS OF AFRICA

Several common themes occur across the diverse myths of Africa: a creation myth in which the creator deity retires into the background after giving shape to the cosmos, a World Serpent, a host of animal tricksters and other spirits, and stories involving twins. All these ideas appear in the mythologies of different peoples – from Ashanti to San – across the entire African continent.

CHANGE AND CONTINUITY

Great changes occurred in Africa during the 1800s and 1900s. Colonial powers from Europe and Asia came and went, leaving the influence of religions such as Christianity and Islam behind them. But many African peoples still hold their ancient myths and religions, seeing them as a rich and vital part of their identity.

THE ROLE OF THE SHAMAN

SHAMAN'S MASK

In a world surrounded by spirits, the most important person in traditional African religion is the shaman. During ceremonies, he puts on a special mask and costume, and through dance and music, usually drumming, becomes the spirit he is invoking. This gives him special powers, such as healing the sick.

CREATION AND NATURE

THE HUNDREDS OF AFRICAN CULTURES have many different stories of how the universe began. One story, which appears in various forms among different peoples, involves a cosmic egg that breaks open to let out the creator god. Another group of myths concerns a primeval serpent, often a python. The world and every living thing in it are made from the body of the snake. African creation myths often involve a supreme god who begins the work of making the cosmos, but then leaves others in charge. People are said to have fallen from heaven, or are the children of gods who came to earth briefly from their home in the sky. Another common theme involves the reasons for natural phenomena – from drought to storms – that affect life in Africa. Most cultures have water deities, to whom people pray when rain is needed.

CAVE PAINTING DEPICTING
AMMA FALLING FROM HEAVEN

CALABASH

CALABASH
The round gourd, called the calabash, is used widely to make containers and rattles, such as those used in religious ceremonies. The Fon say that the cosmos is round like a huge calabash – with the earth floating inside it, like a smaller gourd. A calabash vessel, in two parts, is often said to represent the heavens and earth.

SUPREME GODS AND CREATORS
Most African mythologies have a story about the creation of the cosmos by a supreme god or group of gods. They often emerge from a primal egg. The Dogon people of Mali tell how, in the beginning, a great egg called Amma shook and split open. Falling out of Amma to earth were the creator god Nummo, his female twin, and four additional pairs of Nummo deities. The Nummos created heaven and earth, day and night, the four seasons, as well as human beings.

ADANHU AND YEWA
In Fon mythology Adanhu and Yewa were the first man and woman. When they arrived on earth they had only a **calabash** and a long staff. They taught their children to worship the sky gods and to make sacrifices to them. Then, after seven years, Adanhu and Yewa returned to heaven.

STORM RAM
In Togo it was said that the sun had a market-place. In it lived a ram, which stamped its feet to make thunder and shook its tail to cause lightning. Hair falling from the ram's tail turned into rain, and when the creature ran around the market-place, it made the wind blow on earth.

EARTH DEITIES
Africa's dry climate gave rise to myths about the earth. According to the Fon, Earth and Storm had an argument, with the result that Earth went underground. Storm, believing Earth had taken fire and water, could not provide rain and people suffered. But, eventually, Storm realized that Earth did not have fire and water, so he made lightning and caused the rain to fall again.

VOODOO
The Voodoo religion of Haiti is partly derived from cults brought there by African slaves and is very close to Fon "vodu." Its gods, such as Ogoun, god of war, and Ghede, god of death, "ride" Voodoo worshipers, temporarily displacing the worshipers' own souls. Similar to West African deities, they are grouped into "rada" (helpful) and "petro" (dangerous) spirits.

Peg holds instructions to activate the medicine

VOODOO DOLL

Faces represent Yoruba gods

YORUBA BEADED CROWN

FON CREATION
The Fon people of Benin have a creation myth involving pairs of twin gods. The creator twins, Mawu and Lisa, had seven sets of twin children. They included pairs of gods ruling the earth, storms, iron, and the sea. Each had a special language, known only to the gods and their priests.

Mawu, the moon goddess

Nana Buluku riding in serpent's mouth

Lisa, the sun god

AIDO-HWEDO

NANA BULUKU
According to one Fon creation story, Nana Buluku, who was both male and female, was the most important creator. Nana Buluku made the world, then retired into the background, leaving the control of her creation to the other deities.

MAWU AND LISA
Mawu and Lisa, the twins born to **Nana Buluku**, were supreme deities. Mawu, goddess of the moon, lived in the west and ruled the night. Lisa, the sun god and controller of the day, lived in the east. At an eclipse, they came together and became the parents of the other gods.

AIDO-HWEDO
The rainbow snake Aido-Hwedo, who was created to serve **Nana Buluku**, held up the heavens. The creature had a twin personality. The red part of the rainbow was male, while the blue part was female.

SHANGO
Shango, the Yoruba storm god, was said to have been a mortal king. Because his rule was cruel and tyrannical, his people rebelled. Shango was exiled into a forest, and hanged himself from a tree. Those who remained loyal to him refused to believe that he had committed suicide, saying that he had gone to heaven, sending thunder and lightning as a sign of his anger. His wife Oja became the Niger River after his death.

SHANGO, THE STORM GOD

METALWORKING GODS

Many African peoples became skilled metalworkers. The beautiful bronze sculptures of the people of Benin, for example, have been famous for hundreds of years. For such peoples, the god of metalworking plays a special role. He often assists in the creation of the world, as well as teaching people many useful skills, such as how to smelt ore, cast metal, and beat it into shape.

OLOKUN, GOD OF THE SEA

OLOKUN
The Yoruba god of the sea was Olokun. He wore clothes made of coral, had legs like fish tails, and carried lizards in his hands. He was said to live beneath the sea in a vast palace, and his servants were both humans and fish. Olokun played a major part in the religion of the Yoruba, and was held to be second in importance to **Orisha Nla**, the creator god himself.

GU
According to the Fon, the son of **Mawu** and **Lisa** was Gu, the heavenly blacksmith. His parents sent him to earth to make the world fit for humans. He taught people many of the arts of survival and of civilization, including how to make clothes, how to find food, and, of course, how to work metal.

GU, THE BLACKSMITH

DOGON DIVINE BLACKSMITH ON HORSEBACK

DIVINE BLACKSMITH
The Dogon divine blacksmith wanted to work metal, but he had no fire in heaven. He looked around him and stole a piece of the sun. Then he left the sky and traveled to earth, bringing both fire and metalworking skills with him.

OGUN, YORUBA GOD OF IRON

OGUN
The Yoruba god of iron, Ogun, helped in the creation of the earth. The other gods had bronze tools, but Ogun's iron axe could cut through the undergrowth more easily, to clear a path for the gods. Ogun was rewarded by the other gods with a crown, but he did not want to be a king. Instead, he preferred the life of a hunter.

YORUBA GODDESS OF THE EARTH AND OF FERTILITY

Fertility goddess has many children

RIVER GODS
Most African peoples tell of spirits that live in the rivers. According to Songhay mythology, a spirit called Zin-kibaru lived in the Niger River. His attendants, the river fish, came out of the water at night to rob the rice fields. Other river myths involve serpents or leopards, who expect an offering from people who want to cross the river.

FERTILITY GODDESS
The Yoruba goddess of the earth and fertility was molded by the Great God Obatala (also known as **Orisha Nla**), whose wife she became. She was the mother of **Ogun**, the god of iron. In some accounts, she is also the mother of the Yoruba people, confirming the widespread belief that the people came out of the earth of Nigeria and did not arrive from some other area.

TWINS
The Dogon creation story involves an ideal pair of twins. The creator god Amma and the female earth produced the first beings in the world. Their first child was a deceitful jackal. Their second offspring, a perfect pair of twins, called the Nummo, feared that people born singly would have unbalanced characters, just like the jackal. From then on, they gave humans twin souls, so that they should not be unbalanced.

Twins

DOGON CREATION FIGURE

DEATH
Many African myths say that to begin with there was no death. The Nuer people of Sudan tell how there was a rope linking heaven and earth. Old people could climb the rope and renew their life. Then a hyena cut the rope, the people could not climb to heaven, and so they died.

ANIMALS AND TRICKSTERS

ANIMALS HAVE TAKEN PART in every area of African legend – from the creation to the coming of death to humanity. Often, different animals have roles in similar stories. For example, the Ila myth of the discovery of fire says that fire was brought by the mason wasp, while some Pygmy peoples say that chimpanzees made the first fires on earth. But perhaps the most common role of animal spirits in African mythology is that of the trickster. Tricksters such as the praying mantis, the hare, and the spider are familiar across vast areas of Africa. They are usually creatures with little physical strength who use their brains to outwit their enemies and to win over adversity. They show how, in a region populated by poisonous snakes and such powerful creatures as elephants and lions, it is still possible to triumph if you have intelligence and cunning. The trickster stories are among the most entertaining of all Africa's myths.

Chuku

Dog

Sheep

IBO DEATH MYTH

Snail shell

ORISHA NLA
Yoruba stories describe how the creator gave Orisha Nla (the Great God, also known as Obatala) a snail shell containing soil, a hen, and a pigeon. Orisha Nla was told to go to the swamp and make the ground firm. The Great God scattered the soil over the marsh and put the two birds on the earth. They began to scratch about in the soil, making firm ground.

CHUKU
The supreme creator of the Ibo people was called Chuku (the Great Spirit). He sent a dog to earth to tell people that when someone died they should lay the body on the ground and sprinkle ashes over it. The person would then come back to life. The dog was too slow, so Chuku sent a sheep next. But the sheep got the message muddled, telling the people to bury their dead. This is how death came to the world.

THE FIRST MURDER
An Ifa story tells how a woman put down her baby while she was working, and the child cried. An eagle flew down, spread its wings over the child, and soothed it. The woman told her husband, but he did not believe her, so she took him to watch. But when the eagle appeared, the man aimed an arrow at the bird. The eagle flew away, and the arrow killed the child.

ASHANTI GOLD
EAGLE FIGURE

THE CURSING OF THE BIRDS
The birds were all jealous of the blackbird's plumage, so the blackbird said that he would make them all black if they did what he wanted. But they disobeyed him and he put a curse on them by giving them different colorings. He made the guinea fowl speckled like a leopard, so it would be eaten by leopards. Only the ring dove has a circle of black around its neck, which the blackbird made with his claw.

SPECKLED GUINEA FOWL

Tortoise

TORTOISE AND HARE
Tortoise said that he could jump farther than Hare, but tricked him by placing his wife in the distance. When Hare saw the figure of a tortoise ahead, he thought Tortoise had made a huge jump.

MASON WASP
Ila myth explains the origin of fire. In the beginning there was no fire, and the animals wondered how to keep warm. So the mason wasp, vulture, fish-eagle, and crow flew toward heaven to see if they could find fire. After some days, the bones of the three birds fell from the sky, but the wasp was able to fly up to heaven and take fire from their High God back to earth. In another myth, the San (Bushmen) say that the sacred praying mantis stole the fire.

THE LIZARD AND THE CHAMELEON

Another myth about the origin of death, similar to the Ibo story of **Chuku**, is told by the Zulu people from southern Africa. The Great God sent the Chameleon to earth to tell the people that they would live for ever. But the Chameleon dawdled on his way to earth and spent all his time eating fruit. So god sent a Lizard with a different message – that people should die. The Lizard moved quickly, told the people god's message, and had returned home before the Chameleon had even arrived. As a result, the people believed the Lizard, and accepted that they were mortal.

THE SLOW CHAMELEON

CAGN

A trickster and hero of the San (the Bushmen from the Kalahari Desert) was Cagn, a praying mantis. He could change shape, becoming any one of a variety of animals and could even transform his sandals into fierce dogs, who would attack his enemies. If Cagn was killed when in animal form, his bones could re-form, to bring him back to life.

Cagn changing shape into an antelope

Spiked base of Legba magic object indicates link with earth

YURUGU

The child of the Dogon god Amma and the earth was the jackal, Yurugu. Yurugu was responsible for bringing mischief and disorder into the world, and he was the father of many of the evil spirits of the bush.

LEGBA

The Fon god Legba from Benin was an attendant of the supreme god. Legba tried to do god's will, but his sense of mischief was always getting him into trouble. This frustrated Legba, so he asked an old woman to throw her dirty washing water up into the sky. This made god move farther away from the earth – and also from Legba.

ESHU

The Yoruba god Eshu was a messenger to the gods and a protector of humans. His two roles were linked when he came to earth to tell people that they had displeased the gods in some way. Although he was a guardian of the human race, he was also a trickster, who liked to confuse humanity.

Tapper used to summon Eshu

THE SPIDER TRICKSTER

The spider Anansi was one of the most famous trickster spirits of West Africa. Anansi was born a man, but was kicked into a thousand pieces because of one of his cunning tricks – this is why he is found as a spider, all over the house. The spider-man Anansi could trick even the gods.

Hornets in gourd

NYAME

The supreme god Nyame was amazed when **Anansi** brought him all the creatures that he asked for. He said that Anansi had succeeded where many others had failed. He gave his stories to Anansi, saying that from then on they should be called the Spider's Stories.

Leopard

Doll

Nyame, the supreme god

UHLAKANYANA

The Zulu trickster, Uhlakanyana, spoke to his mother while still in the womb, saying that he was ready to be born. Right away, he walked off and stole the meat reserved for the elders. He became famous for playing tricks on his enemies.

ANANSI

Anansi wanted to buy the sky god **Nyame**'s stories. The sky god said that Anansi must capture the python, the leopard, the hornet swarm, and Mmoatia the spirit. Anansi and his wife Aso tricked the python, by tying him to a branch with twine. Then they trapped the hornets in a gourd, caught the leopard in a pit, and caught the spirit by tricking her into slapping a doll that they had smeared with gum.

Python tied to branch by Anansi and Nyame

AUSTRALASIA AND OCEANIA

The Aboriginal people of Australia and the Pacific islanders have very different cultures and myths. But both involve great journeys – the Australian ancestors across the land, and the

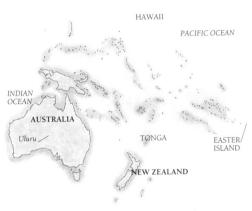

Polynesian peoples over the sea in their canoes, island-hopping across vast distances from Tonga to Easter Island.

AUSTRALIAN MYTHS

Australia's mythology involves the ancestry of the different clans and their Wandjinas (mythical animal spirit ancestors). These wandering ancestral heroes made vast journeys across Australia. Each tribe tells how their clan was involved with part of the hero's journey and how they related to their neighbors. Although each clan has its own myths, the stories are similar.

PACIFIC MYTHS

Thousands of Pacific islands are represented in this book by the Polynesian group, covering a vast area in the Pacific. Many myths have been produced to explain the Polynesian world, both in terms of how the cosmos was created and in relation to how the people traveled so far to arrive on their islands. The spirit world, summoned up by the shaman using masks and drums, is also important in the Pacific.

EASTER ISLAND STATUE

AUSTRALIA

THE MYTHOLOGY OF THE Aboriginal people centers on Dreamtime (or Dreaming). This is a period of time, or era, in which the people's ancestors live, when humans and the natural world took their current form. In Dreamtime, the ancestors took plant or animal form and traveled across the land, shaping rivers, plains, and other landscape features, creating society, and leaving behind the spirits of people as yet unborn. The myths of a particular people, or clan, describe the wanderings of that clan's ancestral hero through their own part of Australia. Dreamtime is not simply a period of past history, but is ever present, manifesting itself in sacred rituals. People become ancestors in the rituals, to reenact their ancestors' past journeys across Australia.

BARK PAINTING
DEPICTING
THE CREATION

UNGAMBIKULA

Two eternal ancestors – the Ungambikula – created themselves in the beginning out of the nothingness. They wandered around the world, as part human, part animal, part plant, and found all the part-created people who lay, shapeless and unfinished, half-transformed from their ancestral plants or animals. The Ungambikula took their stone knives and carved bodies, heads, and limbs for the people. When the pair had completed the work of creation, they slept an eternal sleep.

An Ungambikula carving the limbs of a human

GOANNA

The Aboriginal peoples said that weapons and other useful hunting items were invented during Dreamtime. Goanna, a monitor lizard, made the first bark canoe. Monitor lizards, which can run up and down trees, are especially associated with bark. The story says that Goanna tried different barks, finally figuring out how to make a framework of bamboo and sew the bark to it.

GREAT FLOOD

Aboriginal peoples tell of a great flood, which wiped out the previous landscape and society, to create the present world. In various places, this flood is caused by different beings: a blind woman called Mudungkala; a **Wandjina**; or a great **Rainbow Snake**.

BAGADJIMBIRI

Bagadjimbiri is the name given by the Karadjeri people of northwestern Australia to their two ancestral brothers. They emerged from the earth as a pair of dingoes, before turning into giant men and shaping the first people.

CREATION

The appearance of sunlight is often one of the most important stages in creation stories. In this version, from Groote Eylandt, the east wind thrusts up the morning star into the world, creating daylight. The earth, rocks, animals, and people then appear. Other myths speak of a sun goddess (or Sun Mother) who gives light, so that animals can grow and people can see to hunt them.

DJANGGAWULS

People in northern Australia speak of a trio of gods – two sisters and a brother – called the Djanggawuls. They shaped the landscape by using special sacred sticks called "rangga."

PAINTING OF A
WANDJINA

LIGHTNING MAN

Many of the beings of Dreamtime are associated with rain and lightning. They often carried axes, which are symbolic of lightning. The Wardaman people of Delamere in Australia's Northern Territory tell of the Lightning Brothers, and at Oenpelli are rock drawings of the supernatural Lightning Man, often referred to as Wala-Undayne.

CHURINGA

A churinga is a stone or a board that bears pictures representing events in Dreamtime, but it is much more than a piece of sacred art. A churinga embodies the spiritual power that each person inherits from their ancestor – the soul of the individual. Churingas are considered so sacred that no women or uninitiated men are allowed to see them.

WANDJINAS

The Wandjinas are the spirit ancestors of the Aboriginal people of the Kimberley Region in western Australia. They created the world and named the places, animals, and plants. They came from the sky, with lightning, thunder, and rain. When a group of children offended them, they sent a great flood that drowned everyone except one boy and one girl. They left their images painted on rock faces as storehouses of earth power.

BARK PAINTING
DEPICTING
LIGHTNING MAN

ALL FATHER

Aboriginals from southeastern Australia tell of a creator god called All Father. First of all he made the animals, but they were unhappy – the fish wanted to get out of the water, and the insects wanted to be bigger. Then All Father created humans and granted them all the animals' wishes. The Southern Cross stars represent All Father watching over his creation.

EAGLEHAWK (BILJARA)

CROW (WAGU)

Bark painting depicting two mythical spirits with a sacred snake

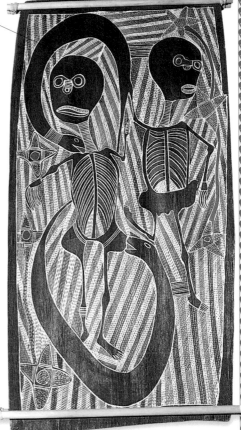

EAGLEHAWK

Crow (Wagu) and Eaglehawk (Biljara) were two ancestors who laid down the rules about who could marry whom. They had a dispute when Eaglehawk refused to give Crow permission to marry the two girls who were under his protection.

CROW

When **Eaglehawk** and Crow argued, Crow killed Eaglehawk's son and tried to blame someone else. But Eaglehawk knew what happened and buried Crow with his dead son. Crow escaped. Eaglehawk punished Crow by burning him and turned him black. But Crow played one last trick on his foe, Eaglehawk, by turning him into a bird too.

ULURU

Rising up magically in the middle of the inhospitable desert of central Australia is a colossal mound of red sandstone. This is Uluru, one of the most sacred sites of the Aboriginal people. Many myths take place there and the rock's lower walls and its many caves contain ancient rock paintings.

RAINBOW SNAKE

There are many stories about the Rainbow Snake, which is a spirit of both creation and fertility. Its curving meanderings created river beds and water holes. When treated carefully, the snake slept, but if it was offended, it caused storms and flooding.

BELL BIRD BROTHERS

The two Bell Bird Brothers were stalking an emu near Uluru when the bird was scared by a girl who dropped a dish of grubs from her head. The girl was turned to stone. Now, when you call out, your voice echoes off the rock as if she were replying.

WAWILAK SISTERS

The origin myth of the Yolngu people of northeastern Arnhem Land tells of two ancestors called the Wawilak Sisters. The Sisters traveled across the land, naming the plants, animals, and places that they came across, such as rocks and waterholes.

YURLUNGGUR

The snake Yurlunggur lived by a waterhole. One of the **Wawilak Sisters** polluted the waterhole, angering the snake. Yurlunggur swallowed the Sisters and their sons and caused a great flood. When the waters drained away, Yurlunggur spat them out. The spot where this happened was the site of the first Yolngu initiation ceremony, where adolescent boys are taken into adulthood.

Whale form of the giant Luma Luma

A soul on its journey to the underworld

LUMA LUMA

The giant Luma Luma took the form of a whale and crossed the sea. He came to the Gunwinggu people in Arnhem Land and taught them how to make paintings and perform dances used in their rituals. But the people killed Luma Luma because he kept all the best food for himself. They left his body on the beach, but he came back to life and went into the sea.

BAMAPANA

Bamapana, an ancestor who lived underground, came to the surface one day to hunt a kangaroo. As he cast his spear, the sun went down. Bamapana experienced night for the first time. He was so impressed when the sun rose again, he persuaded his people to try living on the surface.

DEATH

Many myths recall how an early ancestor's deeds meant that the rest of the human race had to die. According to the Worora of the western Kimberleys, the first man to die was Widjingara. He fought some **Wandjinas**, who were trying to abduct a woman engaged to someone else. He was killed, but came back from his grave. Disgusted by the reception from his wife, Black-Headed Python, he returned to his grave. Ever since, the chance to be young again has been lost.

PACIFIC ISLANDS

THOUSANDS OF POLYNESIAN ISLANDS lie in a vast triangle in the Pacific Ocean between Hawaii in the north, New Zealand in the south, and Easter Island in the east. Before the European explorers arrived, Polynesian peoples migrated from island to island, developing a range of different lifestyles, from the large populations and agricultural societies of Hawaii and New Zealand to the smaller groups of hunter-gatherers on many of the tiny islands. They all developed sophisticated mythologies, with accompanying rituals, which played an important part in people's lives. Because of the role played by sea travel in the peopling of the islands, the theme of beings arriving from across the sea is common. So is the notion of the female earth and male sky, who have to be pried apart to allow creation to take place.

Staring eyes

Protruding tongue denotes power of speech

SEPARATION OF RANGI, FATHER SKY, AND PAPA, MOTHER EARTH

RANGI
One of the two Maori supreme creator gods was Rangi, Father Sky. He held his consort **Papa**, the earth goddess, in a tight embrace at the beginning of time. The other gods were trapped inside her womb, so they forced Rangi and Papa apart. Rangi was devastated when he was separated from Papa, and his tears poured down to the earth as rain.

PAPA
Rangi's wife Papa was the Mother Earth and the Maori's other supreme creator deity. When Papa was cut apart from Rangi, her flesh turned blood red. After the separation, all the other gods fled from her womb onto her surface, where they spread their life all over the earth.

HINA
The Great Goddess of the Polynesians was the moon goddess Hina (or Girl), who took several different forms. In the story of **Maui**, she was the trickster's wife, who lent her hair to help Maui lasso the sun. She could also be Hine Ahu One, **Tane**'s sand-wife, or the wife of **Tangaroa**, whom she left to live with the moon when her husband lost his temper.

Maui fishing islands from sea bed

Sun grew weak, allowing more hours of daylight

Hina

Maui using a rope made from his wife's hair to lasso the sun

MAUI
The Polynesian trickster Maui was born so small and weak that his mother threw him into the ocean, but he survived to become a hero. His many deeds included diving to the bottom of the sea and bringing the Polynesian islands to the surface, slowing down the sun to make the days longer, and bringing fire up from the underworld.

HINE-NUI-TE-PO
The Maori giantess and goddess of death, Hine-Nui-Te-Po, was said to be an aspect of **Hina**. When Maui tried to pass through her body, she awoke and killed him. Since then, death has come to all human beings.

HAUMEA
The Hawaiian goddess of childbirth, Haumea kept an orchard with various trees that grew many different creatures, such as pigs and fish. She was said to renew herself by being reborn again and again.

TANGAROA
Rangi and **Papa**'s eldest son, Tangaroa, was the god of the sea, fish, and reptiles. An aggressive character, Tangaroa was always attacking the land with his tides, and swallowing people and animals with his storms, which took their victims down to his kingdom under the sea. On other islands, he is given the name Ta'aroa and is a creator god.

TANE
The god of forests, Tane helped to separate **Rangi** and **Papa** by growing his enormous trunk and branches to hold them apart. He coupled with trees and plants, fathering all sorts of monsters, such as snakes and dragons, before making himself a wife out of sand.

TANGAROA, GOD OF THE SEA, FISH, AND REPTILES

HINE-TEI-WAUIN, GODDESS OF CHILDBIRTH

HINE-TEI-WAUIN
The Great Goddess **Hina** was also goddess of childbirth, when she was known as Hine-Tei-Wauin. She fell in love with a mortal man and bore his child. The birth was difficult, so the goddess made up a powerful spell that made the birth easier. The spell was still recited by New Zealand mothers in the early 1900s.

PELE

The beautiful Hawaiian fire goddess Pele came to earth and married a young chief called Lohiau. The bringer of lightning and volcanic eruptions, she was said to lurk both in the sky and underground. Pele was quick-tempered and impetuous. When she saw that her sisters admired Lohiau, she destroyed all of them with her fire. In some myths, Lohiau came back to life and married one of the sisters; in other versions, only the beautiful and dangerous Pele remained alive.

LONO

The Hawaiian sky god, Lono, was a peaceful deity of agriculture. He came alive on earth each winter during the rainy season. During the four-month-long Makihiki festival, Lono was worshiped and his image was taken on a clockwise circuit around the Hawaiian islands. This ritual was believed to bring fertility to the fields. At the end of the period he was said to "die," or return for eight months to his invisible kingdom of Kahiki, leaving **Ku** as the ascendant god.

WOODEN FIGURE OF PELE, GODDESS OF FIRE

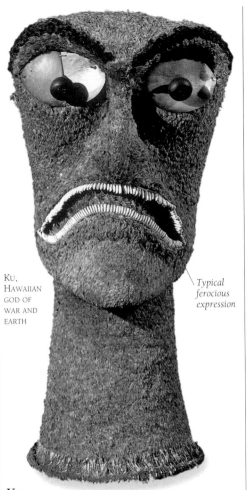

KU, HAWAIIAN GOD OF WAR AND EARTH

Typical ferocious expression

KU

The god Ku (Tu in Polynesia) was the Hawaiian deity responsible for the earth and warfare. He was worshiped for eight months each year when **Lono** was absent from the earth. Ku encouraged envy and quarrels among humans, and was always portrayed with a ferocious expression. But Ku also helped to make the earth, along with the creator god Kane (**Tane** in Polynesia) and his peaceful counterpart Lono.

ORO

The war god of Tahiti was Oro. He relished strife and bloodshed, accompanied men into battle, and could only be pacified with human sacrifices. In peacetime, however, he had a calmer aspect, and was called Oro-i-te-tea-moe (Oro of the spear laid down).

SPEAR REPRESENTING ORO, TAHITIAN GOD OF WAR

COCONUT

According to the Mangaian people of the Cook Islands, the universe was held in the shell of a huge coconut. The great god **Vari** lived at the bottom of the coconut, and beneath Vari was **Take**, a tapering stem. Other Polynesian peoples evolved a similar view of the universe, which was sometimes said to be shell-shaped; at other times it was thought to be egg-shaped.

VARI

The name of Vari, the supreme creator god of the Mangaians, also means mud. People imagined him, at the bottom of the great coconut, as the original material from which all life grew.

TAKE

The Root of All Existence, Take was the stem of the cosmic coconut, **Vari**'s home. All life drew its vitality from Take.

Humans and spirits twisted together

CARVED WOODEN PANEL

EASTER ISLAND

Isolated in the far east of the Polynesian region is tiny Easter Island. The island is famous for its huge stone statues of figures with large heads and long noses, which are arranged on ceremonial platforms along the coast. These statues are thought to be ancestor figures, since much early Polynesian religion was based on ancestor worship. They may represent chiefs of the island, who became gods when they died.

Obsidian eyes

WOODEN STATUE OF MOAI KAVAKAVA FROM EASTER ISLAND

SPIRITS

The Pacific peoples saw spirits all around them. Spirits lived everywhere – from the stars in the sky to crevices in the earth. A Maori myth tells how the spirits come out at night to dance by moonlight in honor of Tau-Titi, son of the Spirit Queen, Miru. Other myths describe spirits embracing mortals, a story that is represented on this Maori carving.

SEE ALSO

INDEX

ACKNOWLEDGMENTS

The author would like to thank:
The team at PAGE*One* for their hard work in designing and editing this book; Neil Philip for generously sharing his knowledge and his library; John Brooks for his support; and Zoe Brooks for her inspiration, advice, and forbearance.

PAGE*One* would like to thank:
Neil Philip for his constructive help and advice; Robert Graham for providing us with valuable research material; Frances Vargo for additional picture research; our author Phil Wilkinson for his patience and hard work; Steve Wooster for designs.

Photography by:
Peter Anderson, Geoff Dann, Andreas von Einsiedel, Lynton Gardiner, Christi Graham, Peter Hayman, Alan Hills, Ellen Howden, Colin Keates, Nick Nicholls, James Stevenson, Michel Zabé

Illustrations by:
Nilesh Mistry; map artworks by John Woodcock

The publishers would like to thank the following for their kind permission to reproduce the photographs:

t = top; tl = top left; tc = top center; tr = top right; cla = center left above; ca = center above; cra = center right above; cl = center left; cr = center right; clb = center left below; cb = center below; crb = center right below; bl = bottom left; b = bottom; bc = bottom center; br = bottom right; bla = bottom left above; bca = bottom center above; bra = bottom right above; blb = bottom left below; bcb = bottom center below; brb = bottom right below.

Jacket:
AKG London: front cover c, back cover tcl: **AMNH**: back cover bc; **Ancient Art and Architecture**: back cover tcr, bla, inside flab back b; **British Museum**: front cover clb, cra; **CM Dixon**: back cover bcr; **E.T. Archive**: spine t; **Mary Evans Picture Library**: front cover tr, tl, back cover bcl; **Glasgow Museum**: front cover cl, back cover crb, br, cra; **Michael Holford**: back cover tc, trb; **Images Colour Library**: back cover cla; **INAH**: back cover cr; **National Maritime Museum**: front cover cla; **National Museums of Scotland**: back cover cla; **Peter Newark's Pictures**: front cover bl; **Werner Forman Archive**: back cover bl, cl, inside flap front b.

Museum Aivi Gallen-Kallela: 86 l, 86 b, 87 c, 87 tr; **AKG London**: Archaeological Museum, El Djem 59 ca, 66 tr, Archaeological Museum, Istanbul 23 cl, Archiv f.Kunst & Geschichte, Berlin 75 bl, Archiv f.Kunst & Geschichte, Berlin 64 br, Bibliothèque Nationale, Paris 71 cl, 74 cr, 77 br, British Museum, London 15 c, 70 tr, Digdiggah bei Ur, Fundort 25 cl, Folk Art Museum, Moscow 14 bl, Kunthistorisches Museum, Vienna 12 cl, Manor House, Rjdigsdorf 62 tr, Musée des Beaux Arts, Lyon 60 bl, Musée des Beaux-Arts et d'Arch., Rennes 66 br, Musée du Louvre, Paris 25 c, 26 ca, 35 c, 59 bl, 67 tl, 71 cr, Musée Guimet, Paris 38 c, Museo Archeologico Nazionale, Aquileia 58 br, Museo Archeologico, Florence 67 b, 77 tl, 126/127, Museo dell'Opera del Duomo, Orvieto 72 br, Museo National de Arqueologia, Guatemala 108 tr, Museum of Fine Arts, Boston 66 cla, Museum of Mankind, London 123 tc, Museum, Olympia 70 br, National Museum of Archaeology, Naples 61 tr, 63 tc, National Museum, Damascus 25 br, Palazzo Salviati, Florence 73 cl, Reuben and Edith Hecht Collection, Haifa University 27 cla, Rijksmuseum, Amsterdam 61 cr, Rockerfeller Museum, Jerusalem 4 cr, 27 c, SMPK, Aegyptisches Museum, Berlin 52 c, Staal Antikenslg. & Glyptothek, Munich 4 tl, 59 bl, 64 c, Teotihuacan, Mexico 106 bc, Vatican Museums, Rome 75 tr, Vojvodjanski Museum 88 tr; **American Museum of Natural History**: 3 c, 101 c, 105 tr, 102 c, 102 tr, 103 cr; **Ancient Art & Architecture Collection**: 2 tr, 9 bl, 10/11c, 13 tl,

14 tl, 17 br, 22 bc, 24 cr, 31 b, 34 cra; 4 c, 35 b, 52 cr, 56 cl, 76 tr, 90 tr, 94 /95, 95 b, 119 b; **Aquila Photographics**: J. J. Brooks 121 tl; **Ashmolean Museum**: 47 tr, 40 b, 49 bc; **Asian Art Museum of San Francisco**: 39 br; Axiom: 86 cr; **Bildarchiv Preussischer Kulturbesitz**: 13 tr, 50 tc, 62 cl, 69 br, 69 cl, Alfredo Dagli Orti 55 b; **Bridgeman Art Library, London**: Agnew & Sons, London 70 bl, Bibliothèque Nationale, Paris 68 br, Bonhams, London 114 bc, 122 br, 123 br, Bradford Art Galleries and Museums, West Yorkshire 92 l, British Library, London 63 tr, 70 cl, British Museum, London 24 tr, 76 bl, Fitzwilliam Museum, University of Cambridge 31 l, 38 br, Gavin Graham Gallery, London 85 c, Hermitage, St.Petersburg 76 c, Johnny van Haeften Gallery, London 73 b, Lady Lever Art Gallery, Merseyside 93 br, Loggia dei Lanzi, Florence 64 tr, Musée des Arts d'Afrique et Oceanie, Paris 118 /119, Musée du Louvre, Paris 21 b, 28 /29, 56 br, 62 br, Museo Archaeologico, Venice 68 cl, Museum of Mankind, London 123 tr, National Archaeological Museum, Athens 59 cr, National Gallery, London 60 cla, 61 cl, National Museum of Iceland, Reykjavik 83 tl, National Museum of India, New Delhi 11 tl, 40 cr, 42 BL, 42 tr, 43 tl, 43 br, 46 r, National Museums & Galleries on Merseyside 59 tl, National Museums and Galleries on Merseyside 4 tr, Oriental Museum, Durham University 38 bl, 41 bl, 128 c, Osterreichische Galerie, Vienna 93 cr, Palazzon del Te, Mantua 63 bl, Phillips, The International Fine Art Auctioneers 59 cb, Pierpont Morgan Library, New York 92 cr, Private Collection 41 tr, 111 bl, 121 br, Royal Library, Copenhagen 8 tl, 82 tr, 84 cl, Stapleton Collection, UK 74 bl, The De Morgan Foundation, London 77 bl, Valley of the Kings, Thebes 18 tr, Victoria & Albert Museum, London 4 b, 39 l, 40 l, 41 cl, 42 cr, British Museum, London 2 cr, 24 crb, 29 b, 34 bl, 35 tr, 35 l, 45 b, 57 tl, 58 c, 108 bc, 122 tr, BM 22 cl, 22 bl, 22 bcr, 23 tr, 48 c, 48 br, 64 tc, 66 cl, 71 bc, 77 tr, 77 tc; Jean-Loup Charmet: 89 tl; **Bruce Coleman Ltd.** 99 br, 117 tr; **Danske Kunstindustrimuseet**: 2 tc, 81 c; **Danish National Museum** 81 c; **CM Dixon**: 26 br, 26 c, 27 tr, 90 c, 90 cr, 90 cl, 102 tr, 115 tl; E.T. Archive: 2 br, 44 /43, 49 tc, 50 br, 56 bl, 60 tr, 60 cr, 61 tl, 61 b, 68 cra, 70 c, 71 tr, 73 br, 74 tr, 76 bc, 78 /79, 113 b, 115 tr; **Mary Evans Picture Library**: 9 br, 12 tr, 40 bl, 46 l, 47 cl, 47 bc, 47 tl, 47 tr, 49 tr, 49 cl, 49 cr, 68 tr, 71c, 81 tr, 81 cr, 91 cr, 92 l, 92 bc, 93 tl, 93 bl; **Exeter Museum**: 114 tc; **Galaxy Picture Library**: Michael Stecker 111 tr; **Photographie Giraudon**: 6 /7, 12 br, 54/55, 69 tl, 71 tl, 74 c, 75 tl; **Glasgow Museums (St. Mungo)**: 40 cl, 41 br, 58 tl, 97 bl; **Sonia Halliday Photographs**: 57 cr, 57 bl, 75 br, 84 tr; **Robert Harding Picture Library**: 112 c, David Jacobs 121 cla; **Michael Holford**: British Museum 1 c, 2 bl, 4 cla, 4 clb, 8 c, 10 bl, 11 br, 16 tr, 17 tr, 20 /21,

23 cr, 23 tl, 25 bl, 27 bl, 30 t, 30 br, 31 tr, 34 br, 35 tr, 50 cr, 52 tr4, 53 cr, 57 tr, 57 tl, 65 cl, 65 cr, 66 cr, 72 cl, 73 t, Horniman Museum 18 l, Hornimann Museum 18 br, Musée du Louvre, Paris 52 l, 56 c, Musée Guimet 37 b, Victoria & Albert 15 bl, 19 bl, 36 /37, 51 bl, 51 tr, Victoria and Albert 51 c; **Images Colour Library**: 2 tl, 48 tr, 84 bc, 84 bl, 85 bl; **INAH**: 13 bl, 106 cr, 107 bc, 107 tr, 107 tc, 108 br, 109 bl; **Larousse**: 87 c, 87 cl, 88 b, 88 bl, 88 br, 89 tr; **Manchester Museum**: 34 tr; **Musée de L'Homme**: 115 cla, 123 tl, J. Oster 108 bl, 109 tc; **National Museums of Scotland**: 16 bl, 108 c, 48 cl; **Natural History Musem, London**: 100 tr, 105 cr, 121 clb; **Peter Newark's Pictures**: 98 tr, 100 b, 101 bl, 103 tr, 104 tr; **National Museums & Art Galleries on Merseyside**: 67 tr; **Ann & Bury Peerless**: 5 t, 42 tl, 43 tr, 43 bl; **Pitt Rivers Museum, Oxford**: 120 tr; **Réunion des Musées Nationaux**: Richard Lambert 39 tr; **Royal Museum of Scotland**: 111 tl; **Scala**: 62 cr, 63 tl, 69 bl, 72 tr; **South American Pictures**: 107 cl, 110 tr, 110 c, 111 br; **Statens Historika Museum**: 83 tc; **Tony Stone Images**: 96 c; **V & A Picture Library**: M. Kitcatt 40 c; **Werner Forman Archive**: 17 cl, 63 crb, 109 tl, 114 cl, 124 /125, Auckland Institute and Museum, Auckland 122 cl, Ben Heller Collection, New York 114 bl, 117 c, British Museum, London 17 bl, 56 cr, 96 cla, 106 tr, Courtery Entwistle Gallery, London 123 bl, Dallas Museum of Art 115 c, David Bernstein, New York 108 cl, Egyptian Museum, Turin 31 c, Egyptian Museum, Turin 30 l, Field Museum of Natural History, Chicago 101 bc, Glenbow Museum, Calgary, Alberta 101 cr, Iraq Museum, Baghdad 24 bc, Liverpool Museum, Liverpool 8 bl, 9 tr, Mr and Mrs John A. Putnam 102 cr, Museo Archaeologico Nazionale, Naples 57 cl, Museo Nationale Romano, Rome 76 br, Museum fur Volkerkunde, Basel 19 tl, Museum fur Volkerkunde, Berlin 106 bl, 110 cl, Museum fur Volkertuunde, Hamburg 106 cl, Museum fur Volterkunde, Berlin 107 tl, Museum of Anthropology, University of British Columbia 16 cl, 103 tl, Museum of the American Indian, Heye Foundation, New York 100 cl, 101 tr, National Gallery, Prague 38 tr, National Museum of Ireland 91 c, National Museum, Copenhagen 79 b, 83 tr, 90 b, Nick Saunders 7 b, P. Goldman Collection, London 114 br, Pigorini Museum of Prehistory and Ethnography, Rome 106 c, Private Collection 15 tl, 117 cr, Private Collection, New York 109 cra, 115 br, 120 br, 21 tr, Private Collection, Prague 120 bl, Provincial Museum, Victoria, British Columbia 14 c, Schimmel Collection, New York 10 tl, Schindler Collection, New York 104 cl, Smithsonian Institute 97 br, Smithsonian Institute, Washington 105 tc, St. Louis Art Museum, US 11 tr, State Museum, Berlin 23 br, Statens Historista Museum, Stokholm 19 cr, Tara Collection, New York 115 bl; **Jerry Young**: 116 bcl